Literacy Solutions

A Practical Guide to Effective Strategies and Resources

By

Jan Poustie et al

B.Ed. (Dunelm), Cert. Ed., RSA Dip SpLD/Dyslexia,
Sharma Cert., AMBDA

(The pages of this book have been laid out with an irregular right hand margin and without hyphenation to aid those with visual difficulties.)

Our two titles 'Literacy Solutions' and 'Mathematics Solutions' share a common core of information. In order to enable everyone to feel that they are receiving a fair deal when they buy both books we offer a discount on the second book purchased. (At the time of going to print this discount was £6. Proof of purchase of the first book is required to obtain this deal, Tel: 01823 289559 for details.)

NEXT GENERATION UK 2000

Jan Poustie

She teaches, assesses, advises, lectures and designs teaching materials for Specific Learning Difficulties. Jan also runs a private practice in Taunton, Somerset under the name of 'Next Generation'.

Jan has taught for over twenty-five years. She has taught a variety of subjects up to and including HNC level. Her teaching experience includes playgroup, primary, secondary and Further Education establishments. She has extensive experience in the field of special needs (including having been Head of a Special Needs Department).

Besides her professional interest in Specific Learning Difficulties she also has considerable personal experience of this field of which not the least part is her own Dyspraxia, Dyscalculia and Attention Deficits; hence her very strong interest in these fields.

She holds the RSA Diploma SpLD/Dyslexia and Prof. Mahesh Sharma's Diagnosis and Remediation of Learning Problems in Mathematics Certificate. She holds Associate Member of the British Dyslexia Association status and her company is a Corporate Member of the British Dyslexia Association. She firmly believes that the only way we can solve the problems caused by the presence of specific learning difficulties is by working together and so most of her books are written in co-operation with various other specialists and national agencies. Her work has been featured in television/radio programmes and magazines.

® Mind Map is a registered Trade Mark of Buzan Centres Ltd.

Warning
None of the medicines/preparations mentioned in this book should be taken without consultation with one's doctor.

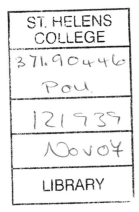
ISBN 1 901544 20 6
1st edition
A NEXT GENERATION PUBLICATION
First Published in Great Britain in 2000
© Copyright Jan Poustie 1998
The moral rights of the author have been asserted.

Published by Next Generation
68 Hamilton Road, Taunton, TA1 2ES

CONTENTS

Acknowledgements

This book has been made possible through the co-operation and/or encouragement of various agencies and professionals to whom I am greatly indebted. Many grateful thanks go to: **Keith Holland** (Behavioural Optometrist), **Rosemary Sassoon** (Specialist in the medical and educational aspects of handwriting), **Hugh Bellamy** (Deputy Headteacher, West Somerset Community College), **Violet Brand** (International Speaker on Dyslexia), **Martin Turner** (Head of Psychology, Dyslexia Institute), **Dr Catherine Caulfield** (Clinical Psychologist at the Brain and Behaviour Clinic, Maudsley Hospital), **Dr Ian Frampton** (Clinical Neurospsychologist at the Brain and Behaviour Clinic, Maudsley Hospital)) **Norma Corkish** (AFASIC ex-Chief Executive), **Denise Caferelli-Dees** (Audiological Scientist and Speech Pathologist), **Madeleine Portwood** (Specialist Senior Educational Psychologist, Durham), **Dr Josephine Marriage** (Paediatric Audiological Scientist), **Mary Nash-Wortham** (Speech Therapist), Rosemary Sassoon (Specialist in the educational and medical aspects of handwriting) and **Patricia Clayton** (Irlen Diagnostician).

I am also very grateful for the co-operation, assistance and encouragement that I have received from the following agencies and organisations and their staff:
AFASIC, The Dyspraxia Foundation, The British School of Optometry, The AD/HD Family Support Group UK, the Dyslexia Institute, the Division of Educational and Child Psychology of the British Psychological Society, the Fragile-X Society and The Hyperactive Children's Support Group.

Many thanks to my friends and colleagues who have supported and encouraged me all along the way and especially to Mary Coyle and Pam Brooks. Thanks also to my lovely daughters – a source of continual pleasure and delight through whom I have learnt so much. Finally, thanks to all my students in the past and present, and the parents of the children that I teach, who have contributed to my knowledge.

The views expressed by the author are her own and do not necessarily represent those who have contributed to, or assisted with, the writing of this book.

Jan Poustie

Next Generation workshops and lectures

These have been especially designed to complement Jan Poustie's books and enable those attending to become more confident when dealing with students who have any of the SpLD Profile conditions. These interactive and very practical sessions extend the information found within the various Next Generation titles. For full details of these sessions and available dates visit the Next Generation website www.janpoustie.co.uk or write (including a SAE) to Next Generation, 68 Hamilton Road, Taunton TA1 2ES.

Foreword

Literacy Solutions has been written to help all of those working (or living with) students who have Specific Learning Difficulties, increase their understanding of the range of difficulties which need to be recognised - and appropriate ways of helping. As the author says - "You cannot provide for what you do not understand." She is quite right.

In this field we need to go on learning about the <u>specific</u> learning difficulties our students may be experiencing. A considerable amount of research has provided the foundations for this book - and as Jan Poustie states - "The research continues." We must go on learning about the range of conditions and the effect this greater understanding can have on the future achievements of our students.

Thanks to the research and thought that has gone into the writing of this book it will be of enormous value to parents and teachers who read it. The reader's greater understanding of the range of difficulties - and the resources that will help the students overcome them will relieve many of their anxieties and concerns. Literacy Solutions is a rich source for us to draw on .

Violet Brand

A word from the authoress

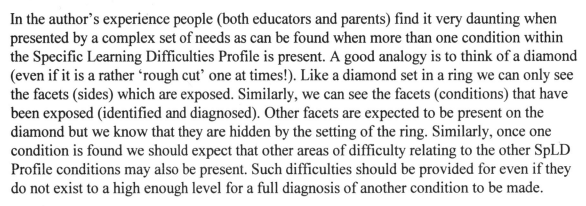

This book has been designed to help teachers, parents and other professionals to enable students of all ages to achieve success in their academic, vocational and life goals. Note that parents are included as professionals here! After all unless the child is at boarding school the parents (or other main carer) will actually have far more experience of working with their children than the educational/medical professionals that are involved with the child. Parents are often a very much underused resource. Much of the practical work can be done at home and many of the physical activities will need to be provided via the parents, e.g. very frequent attendance at the local play park for children affected by Dyspraxia.

In the author's experience people (both educators and parents) find it very daunting when presented by a complex set of needs as can be found when more than one condition within the Specific Learning Difficulties Profile is present. A good analogy is to think of a diamond (even if it is a rather 'rough cut' one at times!). Like a diamond set in a ring we can only see the facets (sides) which are exposed. Similarly, we can see the facets (conditions) that have been exposed (identified and diagnosed). Other facets are expected to be present on the diamond but we know that they are hidden by the setting of the ring. Similarly, once one condition is found we should expect that other areas of difficulty relating to the other SpLD Profile conditions may also be present. Such difficulties should be provided for even if they do not exist to a high enough level for a full diagnosis of another condition to be made.

You cannot climb a mountain without taking the first step. In the same way you cannot expect to provide appropriately for the student with specific learning difficulties without taking the necessary steps to achieve it.

CLIMBING THE MOUNTAIN
Step 1: Learn and Identify
Read about the different conditions within the Specific Learning Difficulties Profile and then identify the conditions which are likely to be affecting the student. You cannot provide for what you do not understand, or only have very little knowledge about. (The Solutions for Specific Learning Difficulties: Identification Guide by Jan Poustie et al, ISBN 1 901544 00 1 was written for this purpose.) You can also attend conferences etc. organised by the help and support agencies mentioned in Appendix 1.

Step 2: Refer
Arrange, in co-operation with the parents, for appropriate referrals to be made for the identified conditions. (Sometimes it is the educational/medical professional who refers and sometimes it is the parent.)

Step 3: Contact
Contact the relevant help and support organisations (see Appendix 1). They help both professionals and parents.

Step 4: Keep everyone advised
Parents keep the professionals advised. Professionals keep the parents advised. Make it a true working partnership.

Step 4: Read and implement all the reports
If you are a professional make sure that you accept and implement the reports received from

outside professionals. Reports cannot be implemented if they are only read by senior staff! Every teacher and Learning Support Assistant who works with the student should read the report as well as the form teacher and Year Head; and a discussion regarding its findings and recommendations should occur between all relevant staff to make sure that it is understood and will be implemented. If the recommendations are not easy to understand/implement, or if you do not fully understand the report, then ring up the professional who wrote it.

Schools can lose reports so parents should never give the original copy of a report to the school – always hand in a photocopy. The Special Needs Co-ordinator (SENCO, also known as the AENCO – Additional Educational Needs Co-ordinator) should ask the staff to initial it when they read it – then the school can avoid possible areas of confrontation with the parents by checking that it has been read by all relevant staff. It is wise for the parent when handing in the report to get the member of staff/school receptionist to sign that they have received it. That stops later problems if the school denies having had it. Schools should keep a record of the reports that they have relating to each student (e.g. on the front of the student's file) as then they will be able to spot when they have lost a report.

Parents have the right to a copy of reports written by local education authority professionals such as educational psychologists. Schools should ensure that parents receive a copy of such reports.

Step 5: Delegate and work with others
1   Some of the provision can be done by Learning Support Assistants.
2   Some can be done in other lessons other than Learning Support. Thus if Dyspraxia is present the PE staff could build in some of the activities for improving neurological function into their lessons. (See Appendix 5: Dyspraxia section.)
3   Some activities can be done by the parents (see Introduction for further details).

Step 6: Learn some more!
The more that you know the easier it is to deliver provision and the less stress you will have when dealing with students who are affected by the different conditions that come within the Specific Learning Difficulties Profile.

Appendix 5 contains a wide variety of resources that you will find useful. As the case studies mentioned in this book show, Specific Learning Difficulties can be overcome. Case studies are a useful tool for they enable us to see that there is hope, allow us to gain an idea of the likely length of time over which provision needs to be given and supply details of strategies that are likely to be effective. After reading this book you may like to read the next book in the Finding the Key to Specific Learning Difficulties Series called 'Successful Strategies for Specific Learning Difficulties' by Jan Poustie (ISBN 1 901544 67 2). It has a large section which consists of a group of case studies. It enables the reader to have a greater insight into the area of provision for students from five years to adult who are affected by a wide variety of different combinations of the conditions which come within the Specific Learning Difficulties Profile.

Stage 7: Support each other.
Just as the person with a broken leg needs support so does:
- The student affected by the conditions found within the Specific Learning Difficulties Profile
- All those involved with the student whether professional, parent or other family members.

Having read this practical guide you may decide that you would like to know more about the products you can use to help those affected by the conditions within the Specific Learning Difficulties Profile. There are a great number of products on the market, many of which may have the words 'multisensory' or 'phonics' in their title. However, not all of these products are suitable for this field. Each of the books published by Next Generation have been designed to provide you with information on reliable and effective resources that can be used across the Specific Learning Difficulties Profile. All the guides in the 'Finding the Key' series include lots of practical down-to-earth advice on how to solve literacy difficulties, whilst the 'Unlocking the Mind' series explain, and provide practical solutions to behavioural and planning and organisational difficulties.

 You may decide that you wish to become better informed about the conditions that are found within the Specific Learning Difficulties Profile. You can do this by reading any of the Next Generation publications, the other titles mentioned in the Useful Resources section of this book and by joining the appropriate help and support organisations mentioned in Appendix 1. These agencies all provide information on relevant courses, lectures and conferences for a variety of groups; e.g. professionals, parents, affected adults and children. Some agencies such as the Hornsby International Dyslexia Centre (London) and the Helen Arkell Centre (Surrey) offer a wide range of courses for both parents and professionals. Further information on training for educational/medical professionals can be found in Appendix 3.

No matter which route you take (conferences/lectures, reading, or training) the accessing of more information will create the knowledge-base and support structure upon which appropriate, and adequate, provision can be negotiated and implemented.

The keys to provision

1. Short & long-term goals

2. Co-operation between all those involved

3. Adjust the methods, materials & the environment

When discussing and implementing provision it is important to remember that the style of provision (and the materials used within it) should be age appropriate and that there should be short-term and long-term goals. This will mean that life skills as well as academic skills will need to be taught; e.g. using a telephone, planning and organisation techniques. The ultimate goal should be to enable the students to function at an academic, social and behavioural level as similar as possible to that of their peers (of similar intellectual ability) and to raise their self-esteem so that they have confidence in their abilities. The younger these academic and life skills are taught the more effective the provision will be and the greater the likelihood that the person will go on to reach his/her full potential in adulthood.

This book has taken three years longer to write than I expected It has been written despite a bull writing off my car, various episodes of flu, severe family illness and a very exhausted author. I hope you find that it meets your needs.

Best wishes

Introduction

Where to start?

This is a particularly difficult question for some people. They may feel threatened and/or overwhelmed by the sheer volume of reports, information etc. that they have to read, understand and then implement. First of all the reader needs a basic understanding of the conditions mentioned below that can be found in people who have a 'Specific Learning Difficulties Profile'. It is believed by many that these conditions are related to each other primarily through the area of language. Thus individuals who have the Profile are likely to have a combination of language-based difficulties which can be seen in any, or all, of the areas of written, spoken or heard language plus that of body language. The appropriate use of language, information processing, understanding and acquiring the areas of language can all be affected. Individuals will have a sub-set of wide-ranging difficulties (e.g. visual, auditory, memory, perceptual, planning, processing, behavioural and communication difficulties). No two individuals will be alike and many will have more than one condition. Associated with these difficulties are atopic conditions such as hayfever, eczema, asthma and nettle-rash. Travel sickness can also occur and this is associated with the presence of certain aspects of Dyspraxia. The following conditions are found within the Profile:

SPECIFIC LANGUAGE IMPAIRMENT (Also known as dysphasia) A continuum of difficulties experienced by children and young people who have not reached expected competence in communication skills in their first language, and whose teaching and learning is consequently affected. Causes difficulties with expressive language (that which you speak or write) and receptive language (that which you hear/read). Often this group is defined by exclusion: 'They are not autistic, the impairment is not the result of a physical, intellectual or hearing impairment...' (Norma Corkish, AFASIC ex-Chief Executive)

DYSCALCULIA Difficulties in understanding, processing and using numerical/mathematical information which can be developmental (there from birth e.g. Developmental Dyscalculia) or can be acquired through the result of brain illness or injury such as Childhood Hemiplegia and ME. It can also be caused by the presence of other conditions within the Specific Learning Difficulties Profile (e.g. Dyspraxia and Dyslexia).

AUTISTIC SPECTRUM DISORDER (Used to be called Autistic Continuum.) Difficulties in social interaction, social communication and imagination-based activities/behaviour.

CENTRAL AUDITORY PROCESSING DISORDER A dysfunction of the processing of the auditory input causing problems with understanding/processing what is heard.

ATTENTION DEFICITS (Also known as Attention Deficit Disorder, Attention Deficit Hyperactivity Disorder and Behaviour Inhibition Disorder.) Causes difficulties in concentrating and focusing attention. It affects behaviour and has several forms.

DYSPRAXIA (Also known as Developmental Dyspraxia, Developmental Co-ordination Disorder, Sensory Integrative Problems, Co-ordination Difficulties and Motor Learning Problems.) There are various forms of it. All of them relate to difficulties in motor planning and organisation caused by a delay/disorder of the planning and/or execution of complex movements; e.g. writing, drawing, speaking, reading, throwing, running etc.. It can affect speech, eye, limb, body, hand and finger movements. It can be acquired (e.g. through brain illness/injury) or it can be developmental (e.g. there from birth).

DYSLEXIA (Has various forms each with their own name; e.g. Developmental Dyslexia.) In the past 'Dyslexia' has been used as an umbrella term for several of the conditions found within the Specific Learning Difficulties Profile. Nowadays it is more appropriate to use this term only in respect of a condition where the main difficulties are with the acquisition of spelling and/or reading skills. "The musician who has Dyslexia often has great difficulties initially with reading music and on-going problems with sight-reading." (Violet Brand – chair of BDA music committee.)

THE FOLLOWING CAN BE FOUND ALONGSIDE THE PROFILE CONDITIONS:
SCOTOPIC SENSITIVITY IRLEN SYNDROME This is a perceptual dysfunction affecting reading and writing-based activities as well as depth perception.

ME/CHRONIC FATIGUE SYNDROME (CFS)/POST VIRAL FATIGUE SYNDROME (PVFS) An illness characterised by fatigue, muscle pain and flu-like symptoms occurring after little or no mental/physical effort. It is usually a long-term illness which can last for several years. Children (from as young as five years) and adults are affected by it. It causes changes in the brain chemistry which result in the person developing an acquired form of the Specific Learning Difficulties Profile.

CHILDHOOD HEMIPLEGIA This is caused by brain damage as a result of haemorrhages in the brain just before birth, at birth or in the first few years of life. Most of these children who have moderate to severe damage are likely to be affected by specific learning difficulties whilst those with mild damage are less likely to be affected by SpLD. There can be difficulties in any or all of the following: reading, spelling and arithmetic. Movement, behavioural, emotional and social skills difficulties may also be present. Two-thirds of these children will be of normal intelligence, the other third are likely to be of less than normal intelligence. Skills relating to non-verbal skills are the most likely to be affected with language skills being preserved whilst visuospatial skills are lost to some extent. Thus similar difficulties as those found in Non-Verbal Learning Deficit can be seen.

It appears that an insult to the brain (e.g. brain haemorrhage) may not always result in the loss of movement of one side of the body. Some children appear to have their physical functioning intact (or almost so) but their cognitive (intellectual) functioning and behaviour may be affected. This non-hemiplegic group may have similar academic difficulties as those affected by childhood hemiplegia. Assessment of their cognitive functioning is by a paediatric neuropsychologist of which there is a shortage in the UK. Referral to such a professional is via the child's GP who can locate the nearest one. There are specialist neuropsychological centres at Great Ormond Street hospital (London) and at The John Radcliffe hospital (Oxford).

NON-VERBAL LEARNING DEFICIT (NLD). "This is associated with a deficiency of white matter in the brain. Such individuals have marked difficulties in the processing of visuospatial information" which will affect symbolic language, geometry, writing/layout, map reading, reading diagrams and the use of planning and organisational tools. (Martin Turner, Head of Psychology, Dyslexia Institute)

This term is being used in some quarters to include forms of Dyspraxia and Childhood Hemiplegia. For further information on this condition read 'Syndrome of non-verbal learning disabilities' by Byron Rourke (isbn 0 898623 78 2 published by Guildford Publications). Bryon Rourke is a neuropsychologist based in Canada.

GENETICALLY-INHERITED SYNDROMES A wide variety of genetically-inherited syndromes exist of which several can include specific learning difficulties as part of their characteristics. One of the most common of these syndromes is Fragile-X. Students who have this syndrome often show marked inattention, impulsive and overactive behaviours which require good student management skills on the part of the teacher. Difficulties in memorising information can also be part of this syndrome. Co-ordination difficulties (which affect writing) and speech and language difficulties (which may affect reading, creative writing and spelling) may also be present to varying degrees. There can be a considerable variation in reading skills which will range from those who are unable to learn to read to those who learn to read quite well. Each student affected by a genetically-inherited syndrome will have a different set of difficulties so the literacy strategies will vary according to the areas of greatest difficulty. Attention will also need to be paid to any relevant research into effective strategies for learning with regard to the particular syndrome which is affecting the student. Thus in the research into Fragile-X there is some evidence which suggests that such students learn to read better through visual strategies rather than phonologically based ones so the picture-based cards 'Dealing with Vowels' published by LDA (Tel: 01945 463441) may be helpful.

AMENDING AND CHANGING LITERACY STRATEGIES Difficulties with memorising information are common in the SpLD Profile conditions and so tutors need to both amend his/her traditional strategies (e.g. the use of a 'word tin' to teach reading) and to adopt new ones. A word tin is where the student has a group of individual words which s/he is given in a small container. The words are written onto a piece of card and the student has to learn all of them before reading the book containing the words. This system totally relies upon visual memory for symbols (letters). Including a picture on each card whenever possible will help the visual learner to have a 'memory peg' on which to hang the word for easier access from the mind but this may not help the non-visual learner.

MAKING THE LITERACY TASK RELEVANT AND APPROPRIATE The majority of students affected by the conditions within the SpLD Profile, or who are affected by conditions which can be seen alongside the Profile, are likely to be under stress in the academic environment. Once under stress one's ability to cope with handling and interpreting symbolic information (e.g. numeracy and literacy) decrease and planning and organisational difficulties are likely to increase. Stressed students need to feel emotionally satisfied and 'tied' to the task and their natural learning style needs to be used by their tutors. Visual students may benefit from using the 'Wordshark 2L' computer package, as its game format makes a pleasant emotional association with the learning material.

The best way of achieving an emotional link is for the task to be modified to suit the student's interests, or at least the task being introduced to the student with reference to his/her interests. Students of all ages can become interested in the task if it relates to their hobbies and they will often cope with an advanced text in such cases; e.g. motorbike magazines. Some students do not have an interest in non-factual information and so story books do not interest them at all. Paired reading of newspapers with relatively low reading ages can be useful here e.g. the Sun. (The tutor reads all the hard words and the student reads the words that s/he can cope with.) Although it must be remembered that all girls are not interested in the same things and that the same applies to boys the author has found that boys can usually be introduced to newspapers via the sports pages and girls can usually be introduced to them via the horoscopes. Adults can instantly be attracted to learning words with 'x' in them if sex is one of the first ones mentioned! The older teenager often quickly realises that he can at last spell one of the most commonly used words in the playground once he has been introduced to the sound pattern 'ck' via 'duck', 'luck' etc..

Research published in 1999 showed that children with Special Educational Needs gained less

 Fragile-X students may find that personalised stories which use the signs in their environment (e.g. shop logos and environmental signs) make learning to read easier. The signs may make the task more meaningful to such students and they also suit a visual style of learning.

'Literacy Solutions' explains some of the reasons for this and provides some of the solutions. A comprehensive explanation of a wide range of different strategies for learning literacy skills can be found in the next book in the Finding the Key to Specific Learning Difficulties Series called 'Successful Strategies' (ISBN 1 901544 67 2).

Once we have this basic understanding of the Specific Learning Difficulties Profile, and its associated conditions, we can then make appropriate and effective provision by following the following golden rules:

1   Raise the individual's self-esteem by enabling him/her to achieve success in a small area in a short amount of time. Praise the individual for their achievement but make sure that the praise is valid. Bright children especially may relate their level of functioning to that of their peers of similar ability so it is no use saying, 'You are really good at that', when it is obvious to the child that s/he is not. However, 'You have really done well, I'm delighted with your progress' is likely to be regarded as a valid comment.

Unless you want behavioural problems do not put a 'sting in the tail'; e.g. 'Yes, you have done well, so *now that you have done it once I expect you to do it every time!'* The raising of the individual's self esteem is an ongoing process which must also occur outside the learning support room/home. In other words the individual must receive praise in the class/lecture room too.

2   Have the individual's vision and hearing checked. (Yes, sometimes it can be that simple!) The bright child with a hearing loss who learns to lip-read early can be missed by both staff and parents. They just moan at him a lot for not concentrating etc.! Short-sightedness is not always apparent to parents and teachers especially if the student's vision slowly deteriorates. Difficulties may only become apparent when at about seven years the school makes greater visual demands on the student; e.g. copying from the blackboard.

3   If either Autistic Spectrum Disorder or Attention Deficits is present then that must be provided for first. (Contact the relevant organisations in Appendix 1 for further details.) At this stage the physical aspects of Dyspraxia also need to be dealt with. Support for physical difficulties reduces unwanted behaviours. An improvement in physical functioning can be very beneficial as a 'knock-on effect of following an exercise programme such as that found in 'Developmental Dyspraxia' is that literacy function improves. (See page A30 for details.)

4   If any form of Specific Language Impairment is present that must be dealt with next with difficulties in receptive language being regarded as the most important cause for concern e.g. the language which we hear and read.

Sorting out the student's provision is actually not that complicated if you use the Golden Rules already mentioned. After that it is sheer prioritisation and deciding who can do what. The wise professional makes full use of the child's parents, or other main carer; e.g.

- The tutor may wish to use the student's spelling errors as a basis for tuition. He could ask the parents to look at the student's book and write down all the words that have been spelt incorrectly.

Sorting out and providing for the individual's problems is much like sorting out a ball of wool once a kitten has 'played with it' for an hour! Find the first end (by identifying the likely cause/s of the problems and referring for diagnosis) and then bit by bit sort out the elements of provision.

- If the parents do not have literacy problems ask them to read the 'Solutions for Specific Learning Difficulties: Identification Guide' (ISBN 1 901544 00 1) when concerns regarding the student's functioning are first raised. The parents can then be part of the identification process and both professionals and parents will be enabled to 'talk the same language' when discussing referrals, diagnosis, reports and provision. The parent's participation may also make the process of identification faster as they may be aware of difficulties other than those that the teacher sees in the classroom.

- If Dyspraxia is present the parents could be asked to take their child to extra swimming and music lessons and to follow the Portwood Programme with him./her (Details of this programme are found in 'Developmental Dyspraxia'; see Appendix 5 – Dyspraxia section).

- The parents could be asked to create a scrapbook with the child when s/he is on holiday and then the tutor can use the scrapbook in future lessons with the child as a basis for stories, sound patterns etc..

- If your local public library offers this service free then sign the appropriate form and ask the parents to enrol the child in their local recording library so that the child can obtain free loans of audio tapes to improve his vocabulary etc..

PRAISE

The student (and all those working with him/her) should receive a minimum of eight positive (good) comments for each negative (bad) one. So, if a person feels unable to give the eight positive comments then they should not give the one negative one! The result of professionals ignoring this ratio between praise and criticism is likely to be reduction in, or a continued poor standard of work, and/or behaviour, and a poor relationship with the parent.

At home the praise can be in the form of 'I love you' and a cuddle/stroke of hair etc.. At school an acknowledgement of a new/tidy hairstyle, politeness ('Could you hold the door for me' followed by a sincerely meant 'Thank-you' rather than a mumbled one!), housepoints/ stars for effort etc.. House point/star goals should be both obtainable and concrete; e.g. be able to be held in the hand.

One parent was very disappointed when her daughters' secondary school changed its credit system. It used to give a slip of paper to the student as a credit for good work. These were presented to the child by the head of year during assembly so praise was seen to be given and the child had something in her hand to put in a file, show mum, dad etc.. The system was changed to recording credits by putting a tick in a box and the member of staff initialling it. Once the student achieved forty credits then a gold leaf was presented to the child.

We all need far more praise than we receive. Praise is likely to be more effective (and accepted by the student) if it meets his/her learning style so we need to use the three senses when giving it:
- **Vision** (put it on the wall, give it in front of others)
- **Hearing** (speak meaningful words of praise)
- **Action** (shake hands & have something to hold; e.g. a certificate, a hug from the parent etc.)

This system went from concrete (a slip of paper and verbal praise in front of the whole year) to abstract (a tick). For some children the tick will be meaningless and many will know that they have little chance of achieving the Gold Leaf.

Credits for 'Citizenship' are a good idea as they can be used for a variety of things ranging from good behaviour to raising money for charities. When the author was based in the Learning Support department of a large comprehensive school she had such a reputation for handing out credits to her own students that pupils from other classes used to try to obtain them by asking her for some. What a pity that some teachers are known for 'not giving out' credits and/or other forms of praise!

Teachers need to be aware of the child who is not receiving credits at the same rate as other students and find ways that s/he can achieve them. It is especially important if the child is only attending part-time as can occur with ME.

Case study: Child X – affected by ME
This child only attended school for one lesson a day and so had few opportunities to obtain credits (especially as the teachers of her practical subjects seemed not to bother with giving them). The child was so upset that she could not bear to look at the blank credit record. Her mother came up with the idea that she should cover it with her favourite pictures (Star Trek characters) and also notified the school that this had become a problem for the child.

Senior staff should be aware of staff who do not give out credits and such staff should be advised on how to give praise (including that of credits) and their rate of credit giving should be monitored. It is bad practice to only give out credits for very high marks for that rules out such praise from too large a section of the student population. Students with poor marks may be struggling just to give in anything at all – especially in the case of students affected by both Attention Deficits and Oppositional Defiant Disorder.

The practice of giving a credit for 9/10 and/or 10/10 in academic work is common practice for schools but some students may never be able to achieve such a high grade. The following sliding scale of giving one credit for a group of marks (or something similar) would help all pupils to gain acknowledgement of their academic skill and the effort made in order to improve their academic level. Therefore, such a system based on the top mark of ten is likely to improve the atmosphere in the classroom:
One credit any of the following:

Two pieces of work at grades 8 – 9/10	Three pieces of work at grades 7 – 9/10
Four pieces of work at grades 6 – 9/10	Five pieces of work at grade 5/10.

Carrots work better than sticks!!!!

Many of us do not receive enough praise in our work place but how many of us would stay employed if we received no wages? Our wages are our 'carrots' that make the task of working more bearable. We do not give the student a wage but still expect him to work for us. If the teacher wants the student to work harder, achieve better result, then s/he has to offer 'carrots' (praise/wages) rather than 'sticks' (negative criticism).

Chapter 1

Dyslexia

THE PAST

For many years the definition of dyslexia has been regarded by some people as 'too loose a term' or an 'umbrella term' that included too many variables. We all know that no two people with this condition exhibit the same academic, social and emotional functioning. In recent years the term 'Specific Learning Difficulties' has emerged. At first some people thought that this term meant exactly the same as the term 'Dyslexia'. However, that situation has now changed and dyslexia is now regarded as being one of several specific learning difficulties. (Those of you interested in the history of Dyslexia will find 'How to detect and manage Dyslexia' by P Ott, ISBN 0 435 10419 5, very interesting.)

The author introduced the term The Specific Learning Difficulties (SpLD) Profile in 1997 when she published her first work 'Solutions for Specific Learning Difficulties: Identification Guide'. She, along with many other specialists and educationalists, realised that in fact few people are affected by one of the SpLD Profile conditions alone. These professionals felt that we had to look at the 'whole' person (rather than one element of him/her) in order to provide appropriate and effective provision.

THE FORMS OF DYSLEXIA

> The identification of Dyslexia relates to an individual's abilities with regard to the reading and spelling of symbolic language. In the case of literacy this relates to symbolic phonological language representations; e.g. words and letters.

Various types of Dyslexia have been described in the past (Jim Doyle's book 'Dyslexia – an introductory guide' provides a good breakdown of all these different forms). There is, however, agreement that broadly speaking there are two main types of Dyslexia – that which is acquired and that which is developmental.

Acquired Dyslexia It is usually found in adults (e.g. through injury to the brain etc.) but can also be found in children through such conditions as ME (also known as Chronic Fatigue Syndrome/Post Viral Fatigue Syndrome) and Childhood Hemiplegia. This form of dyslexia has many sub-groups ranging from Phonological Dyslexia (difficulties with the analysis of sounds and an inability to read irregular and nonsense words) to Direct Dyslexia (also known as 'hyperlexia') where the words can be read but the understanding of what is read is poor.

Developmental Dyslexia This is always present from birth. Again various sub-groups have been described; e.g. Dysphonetic Dyslexia (where the student has problems in building up and breaking apart the sounds in words). Some people have doubts as to the validity of the use of some of the sub-groups to describe the student's difficulties.

THE PRESENT

The British Dyslexia Association's definition of dyslexia as published in 'The Dyslexia Handbook 2000' is:

"Dyslexia is best described as a combination of abilities and difficulties which affect the learning process in one or more of reading, spelling, writing and sometimes numeracy/language. Accompanying weaknesses may be identified in areas of speed of processing, short-term memory, sequencing, auditory and/or visual perception, spoken language and motor skills. Some children have outstanding creative skills, others have strong oral skills. Whilst others have no outstanding talents they all have strengths. Dyslexia occurs despite normal intellectual ability and conventional teaching; it is independent of socio-economic or language background."

The characteristics of Dyslexia are:
- Difficulties in using, understanding and acquiring phonological skills (the sounds that letters make when seen singly or together)

and/or
- Difficulties in being able to remember what a word looks like (and so a word read accurately one minute may not be recognised the next)

plus there is usually a family history of Dyslexia/reading difficulties/the other SpLD Profile conditions being present.

Alongside these difficulties there are also likely to be found difficulties in any of the following areas:
- Short-term memory
- Sequencing skills
- Speed of processing information in certain areas; e.g. speed of reading comprehension
- Planning and organisation
- Directional confusion (confusing left and right is common but other directional opposites can also be confused; e.g. up/down and in/out)
- 'Good' and 'bad' days with regard to literacy functioning (this can lead to adults saying that s/he is 'not trying' as s/he can do it one minute and so must be able to do it the next).

Memory difficulties
These can be found as part of several of the conditions within the SpLD Profile; e.g. Dyslexia, Attention Deficits and Autistic Spectrum Disorder. Short-term memory problems can result in words not staying in memory so that they can be read at the top of the page but have been forgotten later on in the page. Spellings may be remembered one minute and forgotten the next, with the student not being able to work them out accurately from their sounds. Receptive language word-finding difficulties are likely to be present so the student cannot access the word and/or its spelling from memory. When reading and spelling the student may substitute a word of similar meaning or letter composition. Working memory difficulties may also be present where the student is unable to manipulate/process the information that has just been received.

Visual short-term memory
The vast majority of students need to develop the ability to break words into sounds in order to develop good spelling/reading skills. However, if visual long-term and short-term memory are intact (and of a very high standard, preferably excellent) then the student will be able to learn to read using visual strategies alone; e.g. 'look and say' but such skills need to be exceptional for spelling to be correct.

Auditory short-term memory difficulties
Frequently, an auditory working memory difficulty is seen (which is commonly assessed by the student listening to a series of numbers which s/he then has to say in reverse order). This test is commonly called an 'Auditory Sequential Memory' or 'Digits' test. Such difficulties cause problems both with functioning in the classroom (e.g. following the teacher's talk on a topic, processing the teacher's instructions) and with developing phonological skills. The student may find it easy to learn the individual sounds of the letters but may not be able to apply them to words; e.g. can work out 'b-a-t' but may not be able to build the sounds into a word. S/he may not be able to create, or break apart, sound blends such as 'bl' etc..

Classification

Memory is dependent upon access and access is dependent upon the organisation of the information. Students affected by Dyslexia do not appear to have a natural organisational system for words. They may also lack planning and organisational skills in many other areas. The greater the stress that they are under the more likely these planning and organisational skills will deteriorate.

WHAT TERMS DO WE USE – AND DO THEY MATTER ANYWAY?

In some ways the Specific Learning Difficulties Profile term is perhaps the easiest for everyone to use simply because it covers so many areas and describes the 'whole'. Reports from some professionals can be so vague (e.g. co-ordination difficulties, difficulties in reading) that the parent (and some of the teachers) do not really know what they have in front of them. Such vague terms are satisfactory if they are further explained; e.g. as being part of Dyslexia, the SpLD Profile, Dyspraxia etc.. Some reports do not do this, nor do they direct the reader to the main support agencies for the areas of difficulty. Using the term 'Dyslexia' in a report is wise as it is a recognised condition through which students can access funding.

It would be helpful if everybody dealt with the range of difficulties found in this book as a 'whole' and explained to parents, other professionals etc. that the conditions are merely the names of aspects of the 'whole' into which research has been made and for which materials/ strategies have been designed as appropriate provision. We would all then feel much less overwhelmed by the range of difficulties found at assessment and much more able to deal with them effectively.

SHOULD WE REGARD THE PRESENCE OF OTHER DIFFICULTIES AS A REFLECTION OF OTHER SPLD CONDITIONS?

Any of the conditions found within the SpLD Profile can be associated with the presence of Dyslexia. Auditory, visual-perceptual difficulties, spoken language difficulties and motor skill problems are included within the British Dyslexia Association's year 2000 definition of Dyslexia. However, it seems very likely that such difficulties are in fact a reflection of the presence of the other conditions which are found within the SpLD Profile. (In such cases Dyslexia may be an outcome of the presence of other conditions.) This book describes how the SpLD Profile conditions can affect the acquisition and use of literacy skills and so enables the reader to look at the student as a 'whole'. It explains that many of the difficulties in the acquisition of literacy are due to the conditions (other than Dyslexia) that are found within the SpLD Profile. When we look at an individual we see a range of difficulties, with each aspect of the SpLD Profile being represented as a 'peak' (a large problem) or a 'trough' (a small problem or, at this stage in the student's life, not a problem at all). The 'peaks' are likely to be referred for diagnosis and the speciality of the professional that deals with that particular type of 'peak' will determine what the diagnosis is. The following imaginary case studies shows this more clearly.

Case Study A

John is 6 years old and has literacy difficulties. He also has many other problems; e.g. co-ordination and attention difficulties because many elements of the SpLD Profile conditions are present. However, his teachers and parents are very worried about his lack of

 **The 'peaks' and the 'troughs' that are present in the individual's profile both determine which route s/he travels and what the final diagnosis will be.**

imagination and the fact that he is disruptive in school. He argues with the teacher and does not play with the other children. It is agreed that he be referred to a specialist in autism. He is found to meet the diagnostic criteria for Aspergers Syndrome which is part of the autistic spectrum.

His literacy difficulties have not gone away. He still has co-ordination difficulties and the problems with focusing his attention are still present. Later on his co-ordination difficulties may be investigated and Developmental Dyspraxia may also be diagnosed.

Case Study B
Tracy is 7 years old and has considerable co-ordination difficulties. She is struggling to learn to read. She often does not appear to bother blowing her nose, she does not appear to be able to use phonics to build up words and her teacher noted yesterday that she said 'chimbley' when she meant the word 'chimney'.

She does find it a little difficult to get on with other children but will play happily with younger children. Her handwriting is really untidy and she would love to be able to ride her bike without stabilisers. Her mum would like it if she actually used her knife and fork rather than her fingers when she is eating!

Tracy is likely to be taken along a different diagnostic route and may be diagnosed as having Dyspraxia with more than one sub-group of the condition being present. (The indicators in paragraph 1 of this case study relate to Articulatory/Verbal Dyspraxia.) Her literacy difficulties have not gone away and may be of great concern by the time she is nine years old. By the same age people are starting to be worried that she still uses tenses incorrectly and that she has problems with some areas of language.

★★★

The conditions within the SpLD Profile are all developmental (e.g. they are there from birth). So in both the above imaginary cases further investigation might reveal that the conditions by which they are affected are causing literacy difficulties; i.e. a form of Developmental Dyslexia is present.

Some conditions can be seen alongside the SpLD Profile; e.g. ME (chronic/post-viral fatigue syndrome). Here the ME is an acquired condition (it was not there from birth) and so we could say that the student has an Acquired Dyslexia). If the person is one of the 25% of the people who makes a near full recovery from ME then the Dyslexia should no longer be apparent. However, if the individual is one of the 75% who do not make a near normal recovery then s/he will continue to have difficulties of a dyslexic nature. Other difficulties may also be apparent because many aspects of the SpLD Profile are likely to be present, to one degree or another, when the person has ME.

All this can be very confusing for professionals and parents alike because they just may not know where to make a start at helping the individual and which diagnostic route to send the person along. Parents can feel devastated when they read a report that mentions a whole host of difficulties. Professionals can feel overwhelmed and feel that it will be impossible to cope. What has to be remembered is that understanding literacy difficulties is like unwrapping a present (or one of those clever little Russian babushka dolls where, when you remove the outer doll, you find another one and so on until you reach the tiniest one of all).

> **You can see the 'present' (the student's true abilities) if you are prepared to open the 'parcel' (identify, diagnose and provide for the literacy difficulties).**

By now the alert reader will have realised that the more 'layers of difficulty' (number of peaks present) the greater the problem in acquiring and using literacy skills. Teachers and parents will also have realised why methods that work for one student may not work with another. We have to open the parcel in order to see the contents. That opening process starts with identification, progresses to diagnosis and ends when we provide effectively for the contents and its wrapping and we can then enjoy the present! Chapter 1 shows how we do this and the 'Solutions for Specific Learning Difficulties: Identification Guide' (ISBN 1 901544 00 1) explains how we can recognise each of the conditions by their indicators.

OTHER ASPECTS OF DYSLEXIA

It is known that the part of our brain which deals with symbolic information is called the neo-cortex. It is the last part of our brain to have developed as the human species has evolved. When under stress this part of the brain starts to function less well and so we have the classic case of the dyslexic who performs erratically and who when under noticeable stress (e.g. in examination conditions or when asked to read aloud) is likely to perform badly.

The phonological difficulty that appears to be the root of Developmental Dyslexia may have its root in other aspects of the Specific Learning Difficulties Profile relating to difficulties in understanding and using phonological skills (such as Articulatory Dyspraxia, Specific Language Impairment and/or one of the sub-groups of Central Auditory Processing Disorder).

All the other well known aspects of Dyslexia such as short-term memory and sequencing difficulties may be there because of the difference in functioning that exists when Dyslexia is present and/or because of the presence of attention and co-ordination difficulties. Short-term memory and sequencing problems are the causes of many of the problems of those who have this condition and carry on to cause problems in adulthood. On top of all this, what can loosely be described as a 'word-finding' receptive language difficulty may also be present. This difficulty combined with short-term memory and classification difficulties causes the student to have problems with accessing from memory the word which s/he wants to read or spell. This problem is in some ways rather similar to the word-finding difficulties mentioned in Chapter 6. Thus the student can read the word at the top of the page but when s/he meets it again later in the page s/he cannot read it. S/he can spell the word one minute (if s/he is lucky) and the next minute s/he spells it totally differently or produces the same or a completely different misspelling.

Poor short-term memory, classification and sequencing skills are all associated with Dyslexia. This combination of difficulties is likely to make it very hard to even find the 'spelling filing cabinet' of the brain in the first place – let alone try to find one piece of information within it!!

If we think of the mind as a series of filing cabinets we can then realise that the only hope of getting the one piece of information from it that we want (e.g. a spelling or a word) is to know:
• the exact drawer
• the exact file and its place in the drawer
• the exact piece of paper within the file.

Where Developmental Dyslexia is the primary problem there is a chance that a variety of commercial products will work to some degree or another. Some can be used by any adult working with the student; e.g. 'Toe by Toe', 'Beat Dyslexia' and 'Spelling Made Easy'. Professionals and some parents will find that 'Alpha to Omega' (and the associated computer program 'Wordshark 2L') is often an effective tool. 'Wordshark 2L' can also be used by parents to support work being done at school using other teaching systems and to teach spelling/topic word lists etc.. The 'Phonological Awareness Training (PAT) Programme' (Tel: 01296 382868) can also be useful though students (especially the brighter ones) can find it boring to use.

The problem with many of the materials that are available is that they can be incredibly boring because in order to put the information into the long-term memory of these students a great deal of repetition is required via a highly structured system. The brighter the child (and the more qualitative his/her mind; e.g. the more s/he dislikes doing things in a set way) the more reluctant s/he may be to use such materials unless s/he is highly motivated. However, some students really like 'plodding' because they are quite happy just to achieve today's goal and regular small-scale success gradually builds up their self-esteem and their skills. Such students may respond well to 'Toe by Toe', 'PAT' and 'Alpha to Omega'. The student who likes variety may prefer the tutor writing phonological stories based on the student's own experiences and family (Appendix 2 – Method 4). Alternatively, commercial products such as 'Beat Dyslexia' may be suitable. 'Spelling Made Easy' comes somewhere between the two types of work as in each section some tasks are repetitive whilst others are creative.

'Wordshark 2L' seems to suit most students as it has a game format and enables students to concentrate on visual or auditory strategies (or a combination of the two senses) for learning to read, spell and improve dictionary skills etc.. In fact students can become so involved in playing the games that it is difficult to tear them away from the computer.

Memory can be trained to a certain extent, as can sequential skill development. LDA (Tel: 01945 463441), Taskmaster (Tel: 0116 270 4286) and CALSC (Tel: 020 8642 4663) stock a variety of materials to help with these skills but the basic difficulty in these areas will remain. Classification skills can be taught and vastly improved by using games such as the number version of Rummikub® (available from Next Generation and toyshops) and practical activities relating to the classification of shape, size and colour with regard to numbers and letters can also help. In the case of letters this classification process needs to be extended to their sounds and the blends when several letters are put together. Ultimately this process must be taken to the point where the student is able to classify such information using the appropriate ways of recording it. This can be achieved by using Carroll diagrams, Venn diagrams and alternative organisational formats; e.g. Mind Maps, Shape/Picture Maps, Grids and Lists dependent upon the learning style of the student. These recording techniques help to connect the individual pieces of information within the brain and so make them more accessible to the student. (These formats can be found in 'Planning and Organisation Solutions ISBN 1 901544 81 8. This title also includes strategies for teaching classification skills.) Once the information is organised in the mind there is at least a chance that the right filing cabinet will be accessed.

SEVERE PROBLEMS WITH ACQUIRING LITERACY SKILLS
It is when we have several Specific Learning Difficulties Profile peaks and/or the Dyslexia is

Even students with severe difficulties can obtain their goals. Thus at GCSE level they may obtain the necessary five passes at 'C' grade and above to progress into 'A' level work/Further Education. However, the need to spend so much time on the literacy aspects of their examinations can mean that they cannot spend so much time on the subjects at which they excel. Thus they may gain a 'C' in English but are very disappointed that they do not achieve the A* that they were capable of achieving for their best subject.

severe, that we start to encounter major problems with acquiring literacy skills. Various strategies and resources can be found in this book. Information on further resources, strategies for developing phonological skills, writing skills and encouraging the development of reading skills will be in titles published by Next Generation over the coming two years. (Those readers who wish to keep up-to-date with our publications can be put onto our electronic mailing list by sending their e-mail details to jan.poustie@virgin.net)

Even students with severe Dyslexia (whatever its cause) can usually be taught to read – though specialist intervention is needed and the earlier that the provision is started the greater the likelihood of success. Once they learn to read these students are likely to find reading tasks very tiring and often frustrating. Their reading accuracy may deteriorate quite quickly so that by the end of the page/chapter/examination they are functioning poorly. They may read so slowly that they often do not get enough practice at reading to develop a good reading speed. For the same reason they may not develop advanced reading techniques such as scanning of text which are so necessary when they have to research written information for public examinations and in the workplace.

What they need is time – time to sit and read information that interests them. All too often their only reading experience during their school years is material that they have to read and so they never find pleasure in the task. Some students are lucky and a love of reading is given to them by a tutor/parent or is in-built in them. Others only find a pleasure in reading well after they have left school when there is more time of an evening and a weekend to relax with a book or more commonly a magazine relating to their interests; e.g. car magazines. Some may never develop the skill well enough for it to be a useful tool to them. Instead they learn information via videos, television, audio tapes and through the medium of electronic aids which read information to them.

Writing: A variety of talking word processors are available for the various types of computer; e.g. Acorn & PC. We now have available voice-activated programs where the student dictates to the computer which then puts the words on screen. Another type of program can be used to read the words out loud to the student. Mark College (Somerset, Tel: 01278 641632) arranges courses where students can try out such technology.) Predictive lexicon programs can guess what the student wants to type next and saves him/her having to press more than one key for even a long word. A variety of predictive lexicon programs exist,; some operate under Windows 3.1 and '95 whilst others are for more modern versions of Windows. 'Prophet' is particularly good; other people may prefer 'Co-writer' or 'Texthelp' both of which speak the word.

Reading and spelling: Reading text has now become much easier thanks to a variety of electronic products (such as 'Reading Edge') which are very expensive but can help with the Dyslexia if it is severe as they can read whole pages at a time. Teaching such students to spell seems to be a very much harder task than teaching them to read. Fortunately, for this generation of children and adults technology has progressed so much that we are able to direct them to electronic aids that can make a great deal of difference to the quality of their lives. Franklins produce a range of handheld electronic devices which help with both the spelling and the reading of individual words once the student has typed in the letters. (They

 **The student with Dyslexia may become tired after reading, or writing, only a few paragraphs or pages. By the end of an examination he can be exhausted and may be barely functioning no matter how high a reading age s/he has managed to achieve.**

are available from many High Street companies including Argos). The 'Quicktionary Reading Pen' (UK distributor iANSYST Ltd. Tel: 01223 420101) is suitable for students whose typing is weak or who tend to make mistakes when typing in the word. It works in a similar way to electronic scanners which read bar codes. So the student moves the pen over the word he wishes to read and the pen reads the word out loud. Like some of the Franklin devices it can display the syllables and provide a definition of the word too. Those who do not have access to technology may find the ACE dictionary of use as it organises words by their sounds rather than by their spelling (available from LDA Tel: 01945 763441).

As with all things there is no one solution. Depending upon the severity of the Dyslexia some students by adulthood will have succeeded in achieving high level literacy skills without the need for technological (or other major support). The earlier the identification of the problems and the provision of appropriate and effective help, the more likely it is that this can be achieved. However, for the others who were recognised far too late and were never offered the appropriate provision the situation is more bleak. For them there has to be a compromise between what is wanted and needed and what can be achieved even with support. All too often for this group it is the tale of 'far too little, far too late'!! For all students the consequences of the presence of Dyslexia will affect many aspects of their lives both in and out of school for we do not grow out of Dyslexia; instead we just learn strategies to overcome it. This area of Dyslexia is explored in 'Practical Solutions for Specific Learning Difficulties: Life Skills' (see page A24 in Appendix 5).

It is always pleasing to see the progress of students but assessment of that progress is not always a reliable indicator of his, or her, ability to cope with higher literacy tasks, simply because of the amount of effort which the student has to make in order to achieve such tasks. Research into the brains of those with Dyslexia shows that more of the brain is in use when such students do literacy tasks and this means a greater use of energy. Thus, in an examination situation the student may not be granted a reader because he has too high a reading age but this does not take into account the exhaustion he faces in trying to do intensive literacy-based tasks. By the end of the exam the student may be functioning poorly and by the end of the examination period (which at GCSE level can last for over a month) s/he may be barely functioning at all. It is, therefore, important that we do not just stop at teaching reading and spelling skills but also that we teach how to plan, organise and write the different types of information and the interpretation of examination questions. We also need to teach strategies to enable the student to make the most of any extra time granted etc..

The old saying 'look after the pennies and the pounds will look after themselves' is correct. The right amount of pennies (appropriate provision based upon the SpLD conditions that are present) means that the 'pounds' (the student's goals in life) are likely to be achieved. The next book in this series 'Successful Strategies for Specific Learning Difficulties' (ISBN1 901544 67 2) looks at how we go on to achieve the pounds – it includes a series of case studies which illustrate how students affected by different combinations of SpLD Profile conditions can be helped to achieve their goals. The rest of this book provides strategies on achieving the 'pennies'; i.e. how we can help students develop their literacy skills no matter which of the Specific Learning Difficulties Profile conditions are present.

 **Technology has made incredible advances in recent years and for many students it is the technology of the present and the future that will provide some of the support that they need in school and much of the support that they need in adulthood.**

Chapter 2

How the different SpLD Profile conditions can affect literacy skills

There is now general recognition that a number of conditions are commonly being seen together in various combinations. These conditions (which are believed to be related to each other primarily through the area of language) can be referred to as the Specific Learning Difficulty Profile. (Details of the Profile can found on pages 1 and 2.)

WHAT FACTORS HAVE CAUSED THE SpLD PROFILE TO EMERGE?
1. People are looking beyond the horizons of their own discipline/interests to learn about (and recognise) other conditions.
2. The advance of research has caused definitions of conditions to both change and widen. The subsequent realisation that some of the characteristics (indicators of a condition) are shared by more than one condition has caused 'grey areas' to emerge between them.

HOW CAN THE PRESENCE OF MORE THAN ONE CONDITION BE RECOGNISED?
Each of the conditions within the Specific Learning Difficulties (SpLD) Profile affect the learning and/or behaviour of the person in a different way. These characteristics (or indicators) enable the onlooker to recognise the presence of the condition. *(These indicators are dealt with in great detail in the 'Solutions for Specific Learning Difficulties: Identification Guide'.)*

WHAT ARE THE IMPLICATIONS OF RECOGNISING A COMBINATION OF CONDITIONS?
A combination of conditions such as Dyslexia and Dyspraxia can have quite wide-ranging implications for the learner. If, for instance, Occulomotor Dyspraxia is present then a concentration on teaching the rules of spelling is only going to achieve so much but that, and the provision for the Dyspraxia, will achieve so much more. As each of the conditions within the Specific Learning Difficulty Profile can affect learning, behaviour etc. there is a need to both recognise and make provision for them all.

THE FOLLOWING ARE SOME OF THE COMBINATIONS WHICH CAN OCCUR:
*   Attention Deficits alongside Dyslexia
*   Dyspraxia alongside Dyslexia
*   Specific Language Impairment alongside Dyslexia
*   Specific Language Impairment alongside Dyspraxia
*   Attention Deficits alongside Dyspraxia
*   Central Auditory Processing Disorder alongside Dyspraxia
*   Dyspraxia, Autistic Spectrum Disorder and Specific Language Impairment
*   Attention Deficits alongside Central Auditory Processing Disorder/Receptive Language Difficulties.

 Dyslexia, Dyspraxia, Specific Language Impairment and Attention Deficits are seen alongside each other. So, when we look for one we must look for them all. Each condition can 'mask' the presence of the other conditions. High intelligence can also mask their presence and can itself be masked by these conditions. Thus the highly intelligent student who has one, or more, of these conditions may be regarded as being of 'average' ability by his/her teachers especially if his/her oral work in school does not reflect his/her intelligence, either because his/her language is affected by one of the conditions or because s/he is shy etc..

It is more difficult to provide appropriate provision when two, or more, conditions are causing the student to have difficulties. The greater the number of conditions the greater the difficulty in providing appropriate and effective provision. It is not always realised that even a very low level of several conditions can result in considerable difficulties in learning.

THE BEHAVIOURAL CONDITIONS

Behaviour must always be dealt with first, as behaviour affects the student's ability to learn. The conditions which have behavioural aspects are Autistic Spectrum Disorder, Attention Deficits and Dyspraxia. It is now known that there is a 'grey area' in the middle of these conditions.

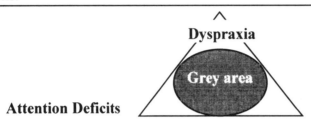

A person may be diagnosed as having one, or more of them, with elements of one (or more) of the others also being present. This is a very new area of research and at the time of going to print no findings have been published. In the UK, at present, provision may not occur until identification/diagnosis is made. Some students who fall into this 'grey area' fail to meet the criteria for each of the conditions and so no provision is made at all for their difficulties.

Behavioural difficulties can create a vicious circle. The student has difficulties in learning due to conditions within the Specific Learning Difficulties Profile. Behaviour difficulties worsen when the student's difficulties in functioning are not provided for. The student loses self-esteem and either opts out (day-dreams, truants etc.) or misbehaves. We break the poor behaviour cycle by giving appropriate and effective provision plus raise the student's self-esteem. Sometimes behavioural difficulties are a reflection of the extreme anxiety which can be found in students affected by any of the SpLD Profile conditions. As such students may lack the vocabulary to explain their anxieties these manifests themselves in behavioural problems which results in the adult resorting to disciplinary measures. This is turn causes more anxiety which results in a downward spiral of behaviour.

HOW THESE BEHAVIOURAL CONDITIONS AFFECT THE RECOGNITION OF BODY SIGNALS AND SO AFFECT LEARNING

Those who have Autistic Spectrum Disorder or Attention Deficits may not be aware of their own body signals. Such students may not associate a stomach pain with a need to eat or go to the toilet. They can fail to recognise the signs of their body being dehydrated (e.g. headache, dry mouth, irritability) and that they need a drink. This can result in the student becoming very irritable and exhibiting sometimes appalling behaviour because s/he is hungry/thirsty, or s/he 'has an accident' because s/he did not realise that s/he needed the toilet.

The student may not be aware of his/her need to use the toilet.

Students with these conditions (and that of Dyspraxia) may have very restricted diets, find it very difficult to try new foods and will not realise during growth spurts that they need to bring more food/drink to school. Students with Articulatory Dyspraxia may be such slow eaters that only foods which are quick to eat (but which may be of less nutritional value) are included in their lunch box. Some students will eat part of their lunch at break-time and then not have enough to eat at lunch-time.

All of these students are likely to behave worse/have greater difficulties with concentration just before dinner-time and can go steadily downhill all afternoon. This is made worse if they only have sugar-based foods at lunch-time. (Such foods only give a quick burst of energy and do not last for several hours as do mixed carbohydrates; e.g. sandwiches, pasta). As soon as school finishes these very irritable students rush home, raid the fridge and the biscuit barrel, flake out on the sofa and may take some hours to recover. If the teacher/parent sees this pattern occurring, opportunities/reminders to eat/drink must be provided if teaching is to be effective. These students may not be able to learn (or may only learn a little) until such provision occurs.

The student's food intake will affect both performance and learning ability.

Students who are receiving after-school tuition may need sandwiches and a drink at the beginning of the session. Initially, many will need a sugar-based snack (e.g. chocolate) at intervals during the session, as the brain uses 'sugar' when it is working and the intensive teaching demands more brain activity. (Note that mixed carbohydrate and protein snacks; e.g. a jam and peanut butter sandwich, rather than sugar-based snacks will be necessary for those in whom sugar snacks cause hyperactivity/behavioural difficulties.) Some schools use a 'withdrawal' system where the student is withdrawn from a lesson for specialist teaching. Students would benefit from being withdrawn from the first lesson of the morning if they eat breakfast, or straight after lunch-time or break, if they are given opportunities to eat during the latter. Always be alert for the student who does not bring enough food/drink to school and so consumes all, or most it, during break and is then extremely hungry/thirsty by the end of the day. *(For further details see 'Practical Solutions for Specific Learning Difficulties: Life Skills' by Jan Poustie ISBN 1 901544 50 8.)*

AUTISTIC SPECTRUM DISORDER (ASD)

If this condition is present it MUST always be dealt with first. This is a very specialised area of provision. Most people do not realise how common this condition is (approximately one in a hundred people have some form of it). ASD is often accompanied by profound learning difficulties, in which case it is usually recognised early, and such students, along with those who have a moderate to severe form of this condition, are usually educated in special units/schools. However, the milder cases (and those who are more able) may go unrecognised and undiagnosed in mainstream schooling. This results in the students, and their parents, becoming distressed and their teachers becoming frustrated with a child that they cannot reach and teach. Much of this situation can be turned around once appropriate intervention occurs but this does require both parents and teachers to acquire greater knowledge of the condition. *(Information on this condition and effective strategies for dealing with it are available from the National Autistic Society – see Appendix 1.)*

 Movement-based difficulties are likely to affect self-esteem, especially in boys where skills on the sports field affect their status amongst their peers.

DELAYED MOTOR SKILLS AND LITERACY

A delay in acquiring movement skills can have a 'knock on' effect on the development of literacy skills. Various factors can cause this delay; e.g. maternal problems during pregnancy, illness during critical periods of the child's development and genetically inherited syndromes/conditions (Dyslexia is known to be 80% inherited and a genetic/inheritance factor is believed to be present to varying degrees in the other SpLD Profile conditions). The term Neuro-Developmental Delay (NDD) is used when there is a delay in acquiring the requisite motor skills at the appropriate age. NDD is believed to be significant in various of the SpLD Profile conditions; e.g.:
- Dyspraxia, Attention Deficits, Developmental Dyslexia
- Central Auditory Processing Disorder (CAPD) – see the 'Solutions for Specific Learning

Difficulties: Identification Guide' for further information. There are a number of 'Sound Therapies' aimed at correcting CAPD which involve listening to specially made audio tapes. Other interventions include learning to sing in tune and to play a musical instrument as these activities can speed up development of certain parts of the brain; e.g. the corpus callosum.

Movement-based strategies can, in certain cases, be very effective for improving a variety of skills as the exercises establish new neural pathways in the brain which enable the mind to work more efficiently. Such strategies can be found in the Dyspraxia section of Appendix 5 of this guide and the Brain Gym exercises on page A27 of that appendix may also be helpful here too.

Neuro-Developmental delay (NDD)
The term was originated by Peter Blythe of The Institute for Neuro-Physiological Psychology (INPP) in 1983 and he defined it as being: "The continued presence of a cluster (three or more) of the Primitive (baby) reflexes which should not be present after the first year of life and the lack of a cluster of Postural (movement control) reflexes which should be present after the first year of life." It affects various aspects of learning; e.g. physical control of the body, auditory discrimination, the ability to follow text smoothly, binocular vision and behaviour.

Blythe (with David McGlown) developed a series of movement exercises (the 'Reflex Stimulation Programme') which the child could do, on a daily basis, at home. The exercises reproduce the movements that a very young baby would make. It is believed that they give the brain a second chance to control the 'baby' reflexes and release the Postural reflexes. Blythe has found that as the 'baby' reflexes are controlled by the brain so the child's presenting problems disappear and s/he can start to benefit from appropriate teaching methods. There are now various versions of NDD movement exercises and another form of intervention is also in use where the Primitive Reflexes are 'brushed away'. 'Brushing' has a long history (it was used early in the twentieth century) and it does appear to have helped some children. However, various professionals have concerns about its use (especially in relation to the vagus nerve) and so it is a rather contentious area at present.

NDD interventions are not generally available on the NHS, though the INPP programme is currently being used in one NHS hospital. The length of the course means that it is an expensive intervention to obtain privately. Some practitioners of these techniques do not charge for a first appointment and advise the parents/adults at this first meeting as to whether they will be able to help or not.

Dyspraxia
This affects both gross motor skills (movements of the whole body and the limbs) and fine motor skills (movements of organs of speech, hands and eyes). Many people do not realise difficulties in acquiring gross motor skills such as kicking and climbing a rope etc. can affect the individual's acquisition of literacy skills. It is also not widely known that the omission of the crawling stage/ crawling imperfectly indicates that there is likely to be a problem later on.

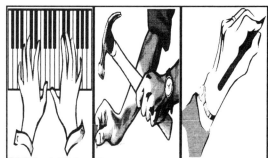
Some fine motor tasks

ADD students often fail to give close attention to detail.

Attention Deficits (ADD)
The presence of this condition can cause the child to not sit still long enough and/or have the patience to acquire many of the fine motor skills. Delayed fine-motor skills will affect various activities such as handwriting, handling small objects (e.g. jigsaws, making models), painting, dressing skills (e.g. tying shoelaces, doing up buttons) etc.. This condition can affect the student's ability to concentrate on stories being read to them and their ability to write for any length of time. So their standard in these activities may not reflect their intellectual ability.

Chapter 3

Attention Deficits

The term Attention Deficit Disorder (ADD) is also used. There are various forms of Attention Deficits; e.g. UADD = Undifferentiated Attention Deficit Disorder and ADHD = Attention Deficit Hyperactivity Disorder.

The presence of Attention Deficits can cause students to have major difficulties in functioning within the classroom and in achieving tasks that require mental effort. Both sexes can have Attention Deficits. Although both twins and non-twins may have the condition, twins (particularly boys) are especially likely to have difficulties in concentrating and staying on task. *(Contact TAMBA for further details, their address is in Appendix 1.)*

Attention Deficits can often be seen alongside Dyslexia and Dyspraxia. These combinations are not always recognised for several reasons:

1   UADD may be present. This is the non-hyperactive form where the person is a daydreamer and usually shows signs of anxiety.

2   The 'Not as Specified' (NOS) form of Attention Deficits may be present. This is where the person meets most, but not all, of the criteria for Attention Deficits. The problems of such students are often ignored as a diagnosis of ADHD or UADD is not given.

3   When the hyperactivity in ADHD takes the form of fidgeting with fingers/hair etc. and restlessness rather than students being out of their seats/moving round the room. Hyperactivity may also be seen as 'verbal diarrhoea' where the person talks 'too much'.

There is increasing evidence that ADD behaviours can be caused by a variety of factors; it appears that each of these factors can result in any of the forms of ADD being present.

- Normally the cortex of the brain dampens the limbic system of the brain. The limbic system is closely involved in emotional behaviour. A chemical imbalance in the brain decreases the dampening effect of the cortex and causes difficulties in controlling one's actions/thoughts. This group appears to respond to chemical interventions (e.g. Ritalin, combinations of drugs) in order to enable them to focus on academic work and reduce unwanted behaviours.

- The reduced number of reinforced neural connections in the brain (that are believed to occur when Dyspraxia is present) result in the limbic system of the brain not being dampened enough by the cortex. This group may respond to the use of dietary supplements (see pages 31 and 32 in this book and Portwood's 'Developmental Dyspraxia' ISBN 1 85346 573 9).

- The cranium (skull) consists of various bones which at birth can move a small amount to allow the baby to pass through the birth canal. This passage through the canal causes

Teaching the student to read first (rather than concentrating on both reading and spelling simultaneously as is common in Specific Learning Difficulties teaching) may well be necessary.

 **Their teachers (parents and spouses) find this group of students very frustrating as their tendency to lose things, and be forgetful, results in them appearing for lessons/activities without pen, pencil, glasses etc..**

'moulding of the cranium'. If this moulding does not occur (e.g. through a very fast second stage of labour, a Caesarean birth) then ADD behaviours can result. The ADD can be reduced by the use of Cranial Osteopathy. One needs to contact one's local osteopath (see Yellow Pages telephone book) to find out which ones have a speciality in this field.

- Elements in the diet appear to cause hyperactivity; a variety of foods including oranges, certain colourings, chocolate, coke etc. can all contribute to such problems. An unbalanced sugar level can also occur so the student has 'sugar highs' just after taking sugar-laden foods (sweets etc.), then does not eat enough/does not eat mixed carbohydrate foods and so becomes hungry and hits a 'sugar low'. Very uneven behaviours can result from this. Modifying the diet can modify the behaviour. However, some ADD students eat only a small range of foods and may be very resistant to trying new foods/changing their routines. Interestingly enough, the author noted that in one child the behaviours were increased when the child had milk chocolate but were not increased when the child ate white chocolate.
- Attention Deficit behaviours in the listening environment can be found when Central Auditory Processing Disorder is present. Once the auditory processing has improved and/or the student's difficulties are compensated for, the behaviour is likely to improve. (See chapter 5.)
- The gifted student can appear to show behaviours similar to those of the ADD student. S/he, like the ADD student, needs a modification of various factors such as the environment/task if s/he is to be anything other than a 'square peg in a round hole'. The importance of changing these factors cannot be underestimated and so these are discussed further in Chapter 9.

No matter what the cause of the ADD behaviours homeopathy can be helpful (contact the Society of Homeopaths, Tel 01604 21400 for local professionals) and an understanding adult who can help the student to talk through the situations that stress him/her may be essential. Of course some students may be affected by many of the causal factors mentioned above; e.g. a gifted student affected by Dyspraxia and CAPD. Strategies for each aspect of functioning will need to be put into place if better behaviours are to occur.

LEARNING AND ATTENTION DEFICITS

When Attention Deficits is present students often fail to give close attention to detail and may make careless mistakes. Thus they are not likely to learn to spell with any ease. Those affected by ADHD (and Dyspraxia) often need to fidget/move around. These difficulties plus their problems in sustaining their attention mean that it is less likely that they will sit with a book for very long unless reading really interests them. Their problems with starting/ finishing work and being distracted from their task mean that if one is lucky they will sit down and start the task, and if one is even luckier they may actually complete it!! Often they are likely to concentrate only on one part of a project and ignore the rest. The completion of the whole task may be beyond them without someone encouraging, coaching and guiding them. Students who are global/qualitative learners (who see things 'as wholes') will find completion of projects etc. especially difficult.

Qualitative learners are like grasshoppers who move from one aspect of a task to another in random order. They prefer to work on the 'whole' rather the elements of the task/project. Some will find it very difficult to see the individual elements/steps which make up the task. Others find it very difficult to maintain motivation once they have gone beyond the initial 'whole concept/idea'. They can distinctly dislike and/or find it very frustrating, boring, tiring and difficult to focus on the 'petty' parts of the task e.g. proof reading, or, the fiddly bits of creating an index and so never complete the task. Those of you who spot the printing and layout errors that, no doubt, will escape the eye of the author (and know how much she hates the final 'fiddly' stage of writing a book) will not be surprised to learn that she has Attention Deficits!

When Attention Deficits is present the student's common dislike/avoidance of tasks which involve sustained mental effort makes all literacy tasks hard work. However, once these difficulties have been reduced/overcome and a motivating force (e.g. that of developing a strong interest in a subject) has appeared there is a chance that these students will work intensively to overcome their problems. Their distractibility and forgetfulness can cause problems in and out of lessons. If one is very unlucky such students will become distracted on the way to a lesson and this combined with a poor time sense may mean that they never appear for it!

The endless restlessness/fidgeting/desk tapping etc. of the ADHD child angers many of those adults around him, especially when repeated requests/instructions to stop it have no effect. Encouraging the child to quietly tap his leg at least reduces the noise of the 'desk tapper'. The frequent verbal and physical interruptions in the lesson, the need to say their piece (before they forget it) and the need to have their turn NOW are also frustrating for all concerned. The frustration can be further increased (and the student can further waste class time) when the teacher 'loses the thread' of what s/he is discussing because the student interrupts once too often.

The effects of Attention Deficits on others can therefore be great. However, for the individual affected by this condition perhaps the worst aspect of it is poor memory and the huge effort that is needed to put things into long-term memory. Unless the information really appeals to the student/has an impact on them then it can be incredibly difficult to learn it. Thus, the author can find it exceptionally difficult to remember dates. However, she can remember (with apparent ease) single fascinating facts; e.g. Wall Street in New York was named because it was sited where the original wall to keep out the Red Indians stood - unfortunately, such facts are not much use unless one is playing Trivial Pursuit!

 **The Attention Deficit student may be so disgusted with his/her work that s/he tears it up in temper/ disgust, or damages the tool that is being used to write the text!**

Strategies that suit these students' natural learning style must be used when revising for examinations. For six years after the author gained her degree she had recurrent nightmares where she dreamed that she had failed her exams. These were caused as a result of the stress of having to overwork to the extent of only having two hours sleep a night for over six months in order to push enough information into her memory. Even then she could only put half her course into memory. During her GCSE work she had realised that some types of questions came up more than others and so had only revised part of the course. During her degree revision she had to use the same strategy, as she knew that it was impossible for her to revise the whole course. If only she had known about Mind Mapping as a revision technique then (see Planning & Organisation section of Appendix 5)! Short-term memory difficulties are also likely to be present with we see Attention Deficits. Such difficulties affect many classroom activities; e.g. copying from the blackboard (a task which can take Attention Deficit students much longer than their peers and their work is likely to contain errors).

It is very much a trial and error process to find a suitable method for teaching literacy skills to this group of students. Finding a responsive tutor that the student likes (and using a system of coaching strategies) is likely to be of the most benefit. (The AD/HD Family Support Group UK produces a leaflet on coaching and information on this can be found in 'Successful Strategies for Specific Learning Difficulties' ISBN 1 901544 67 2.)

Some students within this group may never develop the patience and motivation to learn to spell but will accept the need to learn to read. Teaching them to read via computer techniques can be effective; e.g. Method 4 in Appendix 2. Some schools possess the ARROW system (see page 35 for details) and this may work in the short term but may not work in the long term, either because the student does not feel that spelling is that important, or because accurate spelling requires much more over-reinforcement of the spelling patterns before they will enter long-term memory. The ARROW system suits students who like structure and lots of repetition and so students who do not fit this model can find it fairly boring. Even if a student has already completed one course of ARROW tuition it can be useful to use it as a 'top up' to improve reading/spelling functioning just before important examinations; e.g. in the Spring term prior to GCSE examinations. Generally speaking, the less boring the material/activity the more likely that ADD students will learn the information.

It is easy to assume that ADD students are not trying. What is forgotten is that for these students just settling down to a literacy task may require much greater self-discipline and concentration than the rest of their peer group ever have to use except perhaps in an examination situation.

Chapter 4

Dyspraxia

Madeleine Portwood, Senior Educational Psychologist in County Durham and Chair of the Dyspraxia Foundation's Education Committee, states the following regarding the incidence of Dyslexia and Dyspraxia. *(Note: Comorbidity is the frequency of the incidence of different conditions being seen alongside each other.)*

"Where there is evidence of motor difficulty and perceptual problems it is likely that there is evidence of Developmental Dyspraxia; some members of the medical profession refer to this as Developmental Co-ordination Disorder (DCD). Some medical professionals use neither term and refer to co-ordination difficulties instead. The comorbidity of dyslexia and dyspraxia is high (between 30 – 40%)."

The British Dyslexia Association's definition of Dyslexia includes 'motor function' skills. Dyspraxia can be diagnosed as young as four years once identified by the pre-school professional/teacher/parent and referred to the appropriate specialists. At the same age the likelihood of Dyslexia being present can also be identified. Therefore when 'concern' is raised regarding the child's educational progress in respect of either motor function or Dyslexia the assessment should include tools that can identify the likelihood of Dyslexia and/ or Dyspraxia being present. *(See 'Solutions for Specific Learning Difficulties: Identification Guide' by Jan Poustie et al. ISBN 1 901544 00 1 for further details.)*

Most people who know a little about Developmental Dyspraxia assume that it only affects certain types of movements; e.g. gross movement skills (whole body, arms and legs) and fine motor skills (hands/fingers, organs of speech and eyes). However, it can also affect balance, posture and the way that the student reacts/copes with the environment. The combination of Dyslexia and Dyspraxia can be revealed through the difficulties that can be seen in acquiring skills in reading, spelling and writing. It is important to note that Dyspraxia causes a variety of difficulties depending upon which aspects of it are present. Any, or all, of the following can be present.

POSTURAL DIFFICULTIES

The person may find it difficult to keep in one position for any length of time and be reluctant and/or find it stressful to sit down and read, write etc. for even short amounts of time. Such students need 'movement breaks' where they are enabled to re-settle themselves into a more comfortable position. (Students with Attention Deficits may benefit from such breaks too though they are likely to need to stand up and stretch as well.)

PLANNING AND ORGANISATIONAL DIFFICULTIES

These difficulties are commonly seen in those affected by either Dyslexia or Dyspraxia, with the person who is affected by both conditions being at the most disadvantage. This can be seen by a very untidy bedroom/desk/home, or an exceptionally organised one where the individual cannot bear anything being put out of place. In the long run it is these planning and organisational difficulties (often associated with decision-making problems) which can be the greatest challenge for the adult. *(See 'Planning and Organisation Solutions' by Jan Poustie ISBN 1 901544 81 8 for further details.)*

As adults it is easy to believe that what is right for us is right for our students.
Some students need 'movement breaks' which enable them to find a more comfortable position. Those with Attention Deficits need 'fidget breaks' (a good stretch often helps them to refocus themselves). Adults need to be aware that some students really are far more comfortable lying on the floor when they study and therefore will study better in this position (even with the stereo full on)!!!

SEVERAL OF THE DIFFERENT SUB-GROUPS OF DYSPRAXIA WILL HAVE AN EFFECT ON THE ACQUISITION OF READING/SPELLING SKILLS.

OCCULOMOTOR DYSPRAXIA (MAY ALSO BE KNOWN AS OCCULAR-MOTOR DYSPRAXIA)
"This is a neurological difficulty in ordering, sequencing and acquiring visual information due to a dysfunction in the control and use of the visual motor system." [1] This is not recognised as a form of dyspraxia until the child is about eight years old. Up until that age there may be a "developmental delay in the control and the use of the visual motor system"[2] which is called 'occulomotor delay'. Students affected by such difficulties may be reluctant to look at text, have frequent head-/stomach-aches/feelings of nausea (sickness) during term-time which noticeably reduce during the holidays. They may have considerable difficulties in learning to read.

This condition can result in many difficulties which cause the student to lose his place in the text and/or have difficulties in accurately seeing the text. This causes a variety of problems; e.g.

- Focusing, which affects the ability to copy from the blackboard
- saccadic eye movements (commonly called 'tracking') which affects the ability to move the eyes from left to right (or vice versa) in a fluid movement. This will cause difficulties in maintaining one's place when reading and so the person will omit words, add words, miss lines etc. This difficulty can also cause the letters/words to move around, overlap, swirl etc.
- the white spaces between the letters merging together to form a 'river of white' running down/through the page
- cause the student to construct letters/numerals poorly and present work poorly
- misalign letters/words when writing in columns, grids, charts etc.

The end pages of Appendix 4 provide examples of some of these distortions. They are a good way to show the parent/teacher the problems that the student is having and can also be used alongside Keith Holland's questionnaire to identify those with visual difficulties. Chapter 7 deals, in great detail, with visual difficulties; their recognition and their remediation. *(Further information on these difficulties including the perceptual difficulty of Meares-Irlen Syndrome, also known as Scotopic Sensitivity Irlen Syndrome, can be found in 'Solutions for Specific Learning Difficulties: Identification Guide'.)*

Some of the individuals affected by these forms of visual difficulty may find it easier to learn to read using a computer, as the size of the letters and the spacing between the words and lines can be enlarged so that there is less overlapping of them. (The effects of 'glare' can also be reduced by changing the background colour of the screen from white to a colour that the student finds easier to look at.)

Students affected by Occulomotor Delay/Dyspraxia are likely to have difficulties both in spelling and reading simply because the letters may not stand still/be in focus long enough for them to remember what they look like! Such students may only have an overall impression of a word. They may remember the beginning and last letters (and possibly some of the tall ones in between) but all the 'x' height letters may merge together in memory. Such students may also have difficulties in producing neat handwriting and well-presented work, with laying out words in columns being particularly difficult. They may reverse and invert letters (numerals and musical notation) when writing. Producing maps may also be a problem.

All students with this difficulty will need some specialised input to help them acquire literacy skills. Those with moderate to severe difficulties are likely to need to do eye exercises to train the eyes in correct movements. 'Thinking goes to school' by Furth and

The advantage of this difficulty for some students is that once they have mastered reading they can read the text upside down as easily as they can read it the right way up!

Wachs (ISBN 0-19-501927-X) is an American book which is not widely available in the UK but (if it can be accessed via one's local library) does provide some good eye movement games which can help this condition. Some of the Brain Gym exercises may also be helpful.

The computer program 'Wordshark 2L' has one game devoted to 'tracking exercises' which can be played on-screen and printed out for later reinforcement. (These exercises can be based against any set of words that the student needs to learn.) It also has games which concentrate the student's attention on the shape of each word. There are many Ann Arbor books which are devoted to various types of tracking exercises using letters, words, numbers and music. Xavier produce programs which enable the student to concentrate on the visual shape of the word.

Behavioural optometrists can do an in-depth assessment of eye movement functioning, advise on exercises and provide glasses if necessary. (See Appendix 1 for address.) One's local optometrist can also help by prescribing spectacles fitted with a low-plus lens. This enlarges the text and can enable such students to read much faster and with greater accuracy.

Specialist Specific Learning Difficulty teaching techniques tend to use methods where reading and spelling are taught simultaneously. The ability to read is far more important than that of being able to spell, so for young (primary age) students an effective strategy is to teach reading first and then concentrate on spelling once reading has been fully mastered. (This may be two to three years after specialist reading tuition was started.) This technique is not commonly used in specialist SpLD teaching but it may well be essential if one is to teach the student who has a combination of Occulomotor Dyspraxia, Attention Deficits and Dyslexia.

Students may need each sound blend to be attached to a vowel; e.g. they may not be able to learn 'nd' and apply it to all situations. Instead, they may need to learn patterns by attaching each vowel to the blend; e.g. 'ind', 'and', 'ond', 'und', 'end'. This can be very time-consuming as each aspect of the pattern (e.g. 'ind') can take a thirty-minute lesson to teach, but it is effective. (It is even more time-consuming and time wasting when one is trying unsuccessfully to teach the whole of the 'nd' blend in one lesson and then having to return repeatedly to teaching it again because it has not been learnt, or has only been learnt for a short while, and has not been put into long-term memory.) A technique which can be used for this strategy is to design a series of stories in which the student and his/her family feature. This can be done by designing phonic based stories where a new blend is introduced in each story. *(Story sheets for this have been designed by Jan Poustie, contact Next Generation for further details.)*

DYSPRAXIA-BASED HANDWRITING DIFFICULTIES (ALSO KNOWN AS GRAPHOMOTOR DYSPRAXIA)
(Only a few people will actually have this Specific Learning Difficulty but many more are incorrectly referred for it as the various other causes of handwriting difficulties are still not widely known. See 'Solutions for Specific Learning Difficulties: Identification Guide' for further details.)

This is a difficulty in fine (small movement) motor planning and organisation and control relating to the hand. Other indicators of Dyspraxia can also be present including difficulties relating to arm/ shoulder, gross motor control, posture and difficulties in accurately representing the spatial relations of letters/words. Each aspect of it causes a different set of problems such as difficulties in forming letters when handwriting, applying the correct pressure, writing on the line and writing with an even slant. Students may not know how to 'get the best out of a pen'; one secondary school student was found to be pressing hard with his fountain pen as he thought that this would make the ink come out!

Many people assume that when a student misspells a word it has happened because s/he did not know how to spell the word. What may not be so obvious is that s/he may actually be having more of a problem with remembering all, or any, of the following:

- How to write each letter
- How to join one letter to another
- Where to put the letters in the right place in relation to the writing line
- How to process the information/construct the sentence because of a language/planning and organisational difficulty.

Early signs of later writing problems can be seen at the pre-school level where there are likely to be difficulties with any of the tasks where combined hand/eye skills are needed; e.g. jigsaws, using scissors, construction toys, the fastenings of clothes (e.g. shoe laces, zips and buttons) and using eating utensils. Later on such students, when writing, may:

- press so hard that one can see the imprint several pages down the notebook
- gradually widen the left-hand margin as they go down the page
- produce poorly-presented written work
- reverse/invert letters
- find it difficult to write in a straight line on a blank piece of paper
- find it difficult to keep all the 'x' height letters the same height and/or write them incorrectly through the line, or, as tall as 'd' height letters
- be unable to write using fluid movements
- have spatial relationship difficulties which can cause problems when trying to lay out work, draw diagrams and charts and organise their personal space etc. (Such students are also likely to knock into people/things and will often acquire bruises 'out of nowhere'.)

Using cutlery can be difficult!

Eating food on a tray on one's lap can be particularly difficult. Different cutlery can help. Those affected by 'hyperacusis' (over-sensitivity to sound) may not be able to cope with the sound of the utensils scraping against the plate etc. Students may have difficulties with cutting meat, they can try to cut by 'pressing down' rather than by using a 'sawing' action. Such individuals are also likely to need support in all practical tasks which involve tools; e.g. art, sewing, DT and cooking.

The problems caused by Graphomotor Dyspraxia can be reduced by altering a variety of factors; e.g.

- The writing tool – Some stationers allow you to try out a variety of pens and pencils.

- The penhold – Let the student explore unconventional penholds (as they can reduce the pain and the amount of pressure used). Avoid imposing your own view of what a correct penhold should be.

- Never expect the student to join every letter all of the time – Encourage them to join some letters; e.g. the simple joins (which are from the baseline), whichever joins they find easiest, the very commonest words (e.g. the, and) and always praise their efforts.

- Reduce the student's level of stress (in as many areas as possible) – Help the child to relax (e. g. through laughter, praise and appropriate support) which will in turn reduce the tension in the hand.

- Reduce the stress of handwriting tasks – Enable the student to use a good quality word-processor. Remember that keyboard training is likely to be necessary (though in the future voice-recognition technology may reduce the need to learn such skills). Training and support for both student and parents will be necessary to ensure that the computer can be used with ease. Teaching staff need to provide a safe (and easy to access) storage area for when the computer is not in use. Easy access to a printer and a plug are also necessary! Predictive lexicons (which guess what the student wants to write) and spellcheckers such as the one found in Microsoft Word 7 computer program or the handheld ones produced by Franklins reduce the stress of needing to write whilst simultaneously accessing the correct spelling.

- <u>The paper</u> – The surface tension between the pen and paper can affect the writing quality in extreme cases and so different types of paper may need to be explored. Some people (such as the author) find rough papers difficult to write on and may need a smooth writing surface. Some people may find that they have less control on very smooth papers as the writing tool slides too easily over the surface.

- <u>The writing surface</u> – A pad of paper under the writing sheet is more comfortable than a hard desk/table. A slanting surface can be provided in various ways; e.g. by using a desk that goes on top of the table, by having a sloping desk, or by using an A4 ring binder file as a base for the book/paper.

- <u>Classroom furniture</u> – Ergonomic chairs such as those made by Sebell are available. They have matching desks and are available in a variety of sizes to suit different height pupils. (The student's difficulties will be worsened if s/he is using a desk/table and chair which are far too small/large for him/her.)

- <u>Posture</u> – Time may need to be spent adjusting the student's posture to one where his/her body weight is taken by a combination of the chair and his/her feet which are resting flat on the ground. The ideal posture causes the student to use the least amount of energy possible and the least amount of pain when writing.

- <u>Adapting the student's writing style</u> – It is best not to impose one's own ideas of a correct model for writing letters but to instead encourage the student's development of his/her own personalised script no matter whether it is joined or unjoined.

- <u>Improve the student's ability to spell the commonest words</u> – This will enable the writing of these words to flow with less hesitations needed in order to think about spellings. List 1 (commonest words): and, a, he, I, in, is, it, of, that, the, to. List 2: all, as, at, be, but, are, for, had, have, his, on, one, said, so, they, we, with, you. List 3: about, an, back, been, before, big, by, call, came, can, come, could, did, do, down, first, from, get, go, has, her, here, if, into, just, like, little, look, made, make, more, me, much, must, my, no, new, now, off, old, only, or, our, other, out, over, right, see, she, some, their, them, then, there, this, two, up, want, well, went, were, what, when, where, which, who, will, your. These three lists represent about half of all we read. It is also helpful if teaching staff provide a list of words that are needed for project work etc. well in advance of the topic being covered in school so that the student can be helped to learn to write and spell them.

- <u>Improve the location of the child</u> – Do not sit a left-handed child so that his writing arm can collide with the writing arm of a right-handed child.

- <u>Teach planning and organisational writing strategies</u> – This will help overcome expressive writing difficulties (see Planning and Organisation Solutions page A33).

- *(Appendix 5 provides details of the products mentioned in this section including Rosemary Sassoon's books which provide a wealth of information on strategies for helping with handwriting.)*

Reduce the amount of stress in the student's life at school by redefining the task so that the student can finish it at the same time as his peers. Mind Mapping and other organisational tools can be useful here.
(See 'Planning and Organisation Solutions' by Jan Poustie ISBN 1 901544 81 8)

ARTICULATORY (VERBAL DYSPRAXIA) – THE HIDDEN DIFFICULTY?
Part 1 is an original contribution by Mary Nash-Wortham MRCSLT (Reg.), RSA Dip SpLD and edited by Jan Poustie.

Part 1

The child who has Dyspraxia must be observed and treated holistically, as a whole person, because the difficulties are likely to be spread to a wide variety of dysfunctions including gross and fine movements of the feet, legs, body and arms, hands and finger control. Verbal Dyspraxia may be the only problem for the child, or it may be associated with a range of other difficulties including Attention Deficits and general clumsiness. The soft indicators for Verbal Dyspraxia are those associated with making and co-ordinating the very precise movements of over one-hundred muscles which combine to make the speech apparatus work together to create clear articulations (speech). The speech apparatus includes:

- The lips
- The tongue tip, blade and back which pushes against the soft part of the palate. *(The palate forms the roof of the mouth and the soft palate at the back is vital for speech clarity as it moves up to close off the nasal airway or down to let air through the nose.)*
- The soft palate *(the back of the palate)* closes off the airways within the nose used for blowing, sucking, swallowing and for speaking the 'm'/'n' and 'ng' sounds. It is also used for resonance and tone of voice.

The voice is created in the central neck region of the larynx, which again depends upon the muscles controlling breath. (The breath has to be both sufficient and controlled enough to synchronise the air passing through the vocal folds (vocal cords) in a series of rapid puffs which cause the sound of 'voice' through vibration.

Normal speech is, therefore, entirely dependent upon breath control from the lungs, passing through the vocal folds to make sound. This is turned into meaningful speech by:

- The rapid movements of the soft palate, tongue and lips
- The position of the jaws and teeth
- The resonance of the whole process in the hollow sinus regions of the neck and head.

These difficulties in planning and organising the movements of the organs of speech may affect various aspects of speech; e.g.

- correct breathing for speech
- speed, rhythm and volume of speech ("it may be unusual, distorted or abnormal")
- the way that the voice rises and falls during speech
- saying particular sounds; e.g. 'th' and 'thr'
- mispronunciation of words; e.g. pronouncing the parts of words in the wrong order, omission of sounds, unclear sounds
- sentences may be unclear and/or incomplete.

The student's pronunciation difficulties may not be observable to the casual listener as some students 'mumble' the middle sounds of long words. Unless one listens carefully one is not aware that they are saying the wrong sounds. Students may lose a syllable in long words by 'telescoping' the sounds together. They may also reverse sounds; e.g. say 'lots' for 'lost', and so will repeat the error when writing/reading the word. Sometimes the smaller words can be said but not longer words which have many syllables.

The inability to write clearly is closely associated with Verbal Dyspraxia. This writing difficulty can be linked to:

1. The physical difficulty of actually holding and co-ordinating the fine movements of the writing implement.

2. The (often overlooked) verbal language problem. This can be seen as difficulty with the

actual processing and formation of words meaningful flow of ideas and thoughts:

- From the brain to the mouth (where verbalisation takes place)
- To the writing hand, where the composition takes place as written expression.

Children affected by Dyspraxia often have a history of:

- Delayed onset of speech (or the speech may not be delayed but much of it cannot be understood by the listener).

 into a

Articulatory Dyspraxia has a wide range of associated difficulties

The 'swallow reflex' can be affected. Students may be slow eaters, have had feeding difficulties during babyhood and be slow to learn to suck through a straw. They may have difficulties in swallowing their own saliva, catarrh and have problems in learning to blow their nose.

- A continuing delay in speech (use of words) and language (use of sentences and structure of sentences).

It is not unusual for such children to start single word talking as late as three or four years. Progress may be slow and grammatical errors often persist long into junior (and even into secondary) school.

It is unusual to find a pupil who has difficulty on paper with spelling order, written ideas and order of concepts who does not have an associated, but possibly less evident, verbal language weakness too. Those with excellent visual memories may be able to spell accurately even though they still mispronounce the words and so they are harder to recognise. Beware the silent, quiet, seldom heard pupil, who covers up his verbal dyspraxia with a reserved attitude (and even a stammer) to help prevent the necessity of the teacher paying attention to him.

Part 2

Verbal Dyspraxia is a good example of how conditions overlap – Dyspraxia and Specific Language Impairment. "Early speech and language therapy intervention targeted at the child's main difficulty has been shown to be most effective although children starting therapy later will also progress. Some children will require more intensive therapy and the severity of the difficulty and the motivation of the child will determine this. What is of primary importance is the involvement of the parents (and the other main adults in the child's life; e.g. the teacher) in working with the child on programmes to remediate the problems. Research has shown that children with Verbal Dyspraxia frequently have problems in developing reading, writing and spelling skills. Spelling is particularly at risk because it relies on the breaking down of words into their parts and on making the links between speech sounds and written letters. Many of these children also have motor Dyspraxia affecting their fine (small muscle movements; e.g. the fingers) and gross motor skills (large muscle movements; e.g. the leg). A number of this group will have related specific difficulties with numeracy skills." (AFASIC)

Students with this form of Dyspraxia have to rely on visual and kinaesthetic (movement; e.g. writing) skills to remember the spellings of words. (Their difficulties are increased if they also have a form of Dyspraxia which affects their writing and so can only rely on their visual skills.) They have difficulties in using auditory skills as they are unable to say the word correctly so they cannot 'sound it out' as they write it. This causes them problems with what is called 'phonological awareness'.

Some students can say a word but cannot break it down into its parts either as syllables and/ or sounds. They may:

    A.   not be able to work out that there are two syllables in 'hundred' (hun-dred)

B.   not be able to work out the sounds within the word (c-a-t) and so cannot separate the elements.

C.   only be able to break a word partially. So, they can break 'clip' into cl-i-p but are unable to break up the 'onset' of the word (the initial 'cl' blend) because they cannot recognise/separate the individual sounds (e.g. the 'c' and 'l' in 'cl').

Such students can be helped by phonological awareness packs such as 'Sound Linkage' which enable them to become more aware of the correct sounds of letters and of the sounds which they are 'losing' in speech. 'Sound Linkage' also helps them to learn to manipulate the letters of a word in their head – this skill is essential if one is to become a good speller. Word finding difficulties can be present in students with Articulatory Dyspraxia. Word-finding problems relate to the student being unable to access the word that they want from memory. Phonological awareness training has been found to help those who have such word-finding difficulties.

The student with severe Articulatory Dyspraxia will need speech and language therapist intervention using such tools as 'The Nuffield Centre Dyspraxia Programme' whilst the less affected student will benefit from using resources where they record their own voice as part of a reading/spelling programme. The 'Wordshark 2L' computer program and the ARROW system are particularly useful here for keeping the student motivated enough to practise his/her pronunciation techniques. (The student has to produce a good recording for his use in the games on the computer program and for the dictation exercises in the ARROW system.) The Tok apparatus enables the student to 'hear' his/her speech more accurately and the Edith Norrie Letter Case is very helpful here. (The latter was originally designed by a speech and language therapist to teach herself to read as she wanted to read the letters from her partner who was a soldier in World War 1.)

OTHER ASPECTS OF DYSPRAXIA WHICH CAN AFFECT LITERACY SKILLS

PERCEPTUAL DIFFICULTIES

Various perceptual difficulties are highly likely to be present and visual-perceptual difficulties will affect the way in which the mind processes visual information and so this will affect reading, spelling and writing.

<u>Only seeing the white bits</u>

Dyspraxia can cause students to have this unusual way of looking at text. It is a problem related to whether their brain is prioritising the foreground or the background of an item.

People tend to assume that when we point to a single letter on a card that the student is looking at the 'black bits' which make up that letter. However, some students do not see the 'black bits' but see the 'white bits' instead. As the white background to a letter changes shape according to its surrounding letters these students do not usually progress beyond reading a few words until specialist intervention is provided. The first stage of that intervention is to tell the student which bit to look at! The 'Developmental Test of Visual Perception, 2nd Edition' can be used to determine the extent of the problem. It includes a variety of sub-tests which look at a range of skills such as figure/ground configuration, eye-hand control and spatial relations. (It is available from NFER-Nelson, Tel: 01753 85896.) Trying out different colours of text may be helpful here and teaching the student to write using white text on a black background may also be useful. Referral to a paediatric occupational therapist will also be necessary. *(See Dyspraxia chapter in 'Solutions for Specific Learning Difficulties: Identification Guide'.)*

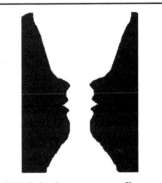

Which do you see first, the faces or the vase? Some of you will find that your eyes keep going from one to the other.

Handwriting is a complex perceptual-motor skill which requires the integration of visual and movement (kinaesthetic) information so difficulties in this area will affect handwriting. Various combinations of these difficulties will cause different sorts of literacy skill acquisition problems; e.g. the student:

- May not be able to interpret and reproduce the angle of a line correctly
- May produce reversals (seeing/writing things back to front) and inversions (seeing/ writing things upside down).

'Developmental Dyspraxia' by Madeleine Portwood (ISBN 1 85346 573 9) is a widely acclaimed book on Dyspraxia which is aimed at both parents and professionals. It contains remediation activities to develop perceptual and motor skills, lots of practical advice and a Motor Skills Screening assessment plus an intervention programme which has been used successfully with both children and adults. A textbook for students and professionals called 'Understanding Developmental Dyspraxia' is now available from the same author (ISBN 1 85346 573 9).

SENSORY SENSITIVITY

Dyspraxia can cause students to over-/under-react to information that they receive via their senses; e.g. of touch, smell, hearing etc. They can find it unpleasant to write when handling the wax crayons favoured when using the Fernald method. (This is where the letters of the word are written in large writing using a wax crayon. The student then says the word and then traces over the letters whilst saying the word/sounding out its sound patterns.)

Students with this difficulty can be distracted by the unpleasant 'feel' of a necktie, the material of their school uniform, the tightness of a waist band. They may not be able to cope if they are placed too close to a source of heat (e.g. radiator, window on a sunny day) or are too cold. They can find the smell of the dinner cooking too unpleasant to concentrate on their work. The teacher's perfume/aftershave may overwhelm them and cause them to feel ill, as can the smell of the cleansers used to clean the classroom. If they are over-sensitive to certain levels of sound (hyperacusis) they may find the voices of their classmates too loud and may find the high pitch of a teacher's voice very unpleasant. They can also find the sounds of certain musical instruments such as the recorder very unpleasant.

The 'fussy' student may be affected by sensory sensitivity.
S/he may dislike certain smells, tastes, textures (in the mouth, or, against the skin). S/he may also over-react when in certain temperatures, especially if the environment is also humid (damp); e.g. the changing room at a swimming pool.

DIETARY SUPPLEMENTS AND DYSPRAXIA

Associated movements

Associated movements can be seen when Developmental Dyspraxia is present (e.g. the leg moves when the child kicks a ball but, without him/her intending it, his/her hand moves as well). It has been suggested by Madeleine Portwood that the reason for these associated movements is that redundant neural pathways in the brain have been retained. (Normally, when a baby is learning to hit the mobile in his/her cot s/he will move lots of different parts of his/her body at once as s/he learns to control his/her arm. His/her repeated efforts to hit the ball programmes the brain to reinforce the neural pathways for moving the arm when wanting to hit the ball. Eventually all the other neural pathways which controlled the extra movements when s/he moved his/her arm will be made weaker and should disappear.) The individual with Dyspraxia keeps many of these redundant neural pathways and so the 'message' to tell the arm to move goes along many extra pathways and so takes longer to process and to execute.

Portwood believes that the situation is different in those who have a metabolic disorder. Here the neural pathways are correct but the brain has problems in transmitting messages from one cell to another. In recent years the effects of metabolic functioning upon the brain plus maternal diet and the latter's relationship with significant feeding problems in new-born infants have been investigated. Sixty per cent of the brain is fat and 25% of the fat is docosahexonic acid (DHA). DHA is found in breast milk and it is believed to be an essential requirement during the foetal stage and for the first four weeks of life. (Up until fairly recently baby formula milk, which is used for bottle-fed babies, did not contain DHA but some manufacturers have now included it.) It is believed that the metabolic problem is caused because the individual is not able to metabolise some long-chain polyunsaturated fatty acids such as docosahexonic acid (DHA).

There is increasing evidence from research by specialists such as Madeleine Portwood which indicates that it is likely that in about 18% of the cases the Dyspraxia is being caused by a metabolic disorder. Such individuals appear to need supplements added to their diet in the form of a combination of evening primrose oil and fish oil. Portwood has found that some parents have reported immediate improvements in their children's co-ordination and ability to process information. The author has also had similar reports made to her of improved functioning in some students (and their parents) when taking the supplements but has also found that it has no effect on other students. The present recommendation is that if no improvement has been noted within a fortnight then discontinue taking the supplements. If improvement is noted then it is thought that the supplement will need to be taken for life. There is talk that within the next two years a simple test will be available to determine who is affected by this metabolic dysfunction. There are commercially available preparations which appear to contain the right combination of oils but it is cheaper to make your own combination using primrose oil and a fish oil such as cod liver oil. (Directions for daily intake will be on the relevant packaging.) It should be noted that this intervention **must not be used by those affected by epilepsy** as it may increase the number of seizures.

The newly revised Praxis II published by the Dyspraxia Foundation contains a great deal of information on the management of Dyspraxia (for their address see Appendix 1).

Footnotes:
1 & 2. Keith Holland in 'Solutions for Specific Learning Difficulties: Identification Guide'
by Jan Poustie et al. (ISBN 1 901544 00 1).

Chapter 5

Auditory Dysfunctioning and Central Auditory Processing Disorder

(Full details on the recognition of this condition and its different sub-groups are in the 'Solutions for Specific Learning Difficulties: Identification Guide' ISBN 1 901544 00 1.)

Aspects of auditory based language difficulties were described in the past by speech and language therapists as Receptive Language difficulties (see Chapter 6) and this term is still currently used. In the second half of the twentieth century The Aston Index was published and this assessment tool enabled teachers to assess for certain areas of auditory difficulty e.g. auditory sequential memory, auditory discrimination and so such terms tended to be used by teachers. More recently the term Central Auditory Processing Disorder (CAPD) has emerged. This term is used by audiologists, it seems to cover a broader range of difficulties than the term Receptive Language difficulties and has been divided into various sub-groups.

CAPD can affect the student's ability to deal with information that is presented to him/her auditorally and to understand written text (comprehension). It has four sub-groups and each one causes different problems in learning to read and spell. Two of these sub-groups – (Auditory Decoding Deficit and Integration Deficit) make it difficult for the student to learn using the usual multisensory methods. Those with Auditory Decoding Deficit may not be able to learn literacy skills using a phonics approach. They are likely to suit visual/ kinaesthetic techniques such as the Amended Fernald method (see Appendix 2). Those with Integration Deficit need a gradual introduction to multisensory methods whereby movement and visual memory are trained first e.g. by them mouthing the sounds rather than saying them as they write the words. Once they are used to this combination they can then be encouraged to speak the words (or the teacher speaks the sounds and then progresses to the individual saying the sounds).

The main cause of Integration Deficit appears to be delayed neuromaturation (Neuro-Developmental Delay- see page 18). The presence of Neuro-Developmental Delay can produce a range of auditory difficulties. The maturing of auditory functioning is related to the development of part of the brain called the corpus callosum. Research has shown that this part of the brain may not work efficiently when Dyslexia is present. The development of the corpus callosum can be speeded up if the student learns to sing and play a musical instrument.

> **REA**: The right ear usually receives language-based auditory input better than the left until the child is about ten years old.

RIGHT EAR ADVANTAGE (REA)

Whenever possible the speaker should be talking to the student's dominant ear. Some students may find it easier to listen to music with one ear but may find it easier to listen to speech with the other ear. Generally speaking, an individual is right ear, leg and hand dominant; e.g. they use the right leg to kick, the right hand to write and find it easier to listen using the right ear (so most of us put the phone to our right ears). However, the SpLD Profile student may have mixed dominance; e.g. left hand and right leg. (Non-audiologist professionals can use Sub-test 9 of the Aston Index, available from LDA Tel: 01945 463441, to gain an indication as to which ear is dominant. However, the Aston test advice is for the child to listen to a transistor radio, or a watch. This test is only likely to indicate the dominant ear if only language-based auditory input is used; e.g. the radio is tuned to a conversation.) It may well help the learning ability of some SpLD Profile student's if they are moved to locations within the classroom so that their dominant ear faces the main conversation/discussion areas. A change of location during school assembly may also be useful; e.g. closer to the person who is speaking but not too close to loudspeakers as sounds can be distorted when you are close to them.

STAGGERED SPONDIAC DIFFICULTIES

Listening difficulties can occur when one ear hears better than the other (or there is an assymetry in hearing ability between the two ears). Specialists in this field do not agree on appropriate remediation for such difficulties. One suggested strategy is to aid amplification of the poor ear (using a hearing aid with only minimal amplification and only worn at school). This strategy does not work for all children and some specialists are against its use because it increases the noise level of the speech organ. Some strategies are agreed by all e.g. that preferential seating is always beneficial (with the student's good ear close to the centre of the classroom's activities/area of discussion and away from noise coming through windows and hallway doors etc.).

ENVIRONMENT

Central Auditory Processing Disorder can cause problems for the individual in the busy/noisy classroom and such students may benefit from small teaching groups. The student's desk placement in the classroom is important. S/he should always either face the person who is speaking or have his/her dominant ear facing in that direction. Classroom environments tend to be poor acoustically as the many hard surfaces reflect sound so difficulties in processing are likely to occur in classrooms without carpets. Individuals are also likely to experience greater listening difficulties large acoustically-poor rooms (swimming pools, gyms, churches etc.) and cars due to poor acoustics whilst the older students may experience difficulties in pubs! Such students suit an environment where they are not taught by lecturing but this may be difficult to achieve in a college/university setting. However, some lectures in such environments are now being televised and a video recording of the lecture that the student could watch at leisure would help some students as they could then play it several times until the language was understood. A glossary of terms used in topics given out several weeks before the topic was started would also help individuals familiarise themselves with the vocabulary prior to having to listen to the words being used.

Sometimes students can be told off for poor concentration, daydreaming, or copying from the student next to them. They can be helped if the environment is made as quiet as possible (carpets are best for floor coverings). The individual should sit as close to the teacher/lecturer/therapist as possible. It is best if the teacher/lecturer/therapist speaks slowly and simply whilst facing the pupil. When auditory skills are weak the teacher will need to use a variety of visual aids to help the student understand both the vocabulary and the information being taught. Worksheets with plenty of relevant diagrams/pictures, videos, television programmes and computer programs can help the individual to understand key points – this may be essential if the individual also has considerable problems in reading. The Mind Mapping strategy of showing the connections between pieces of information can also be useful here (see Appendix 5 – Planning & Organisation section).

AUDITORY STIMULATION

Lack of stimulation appears to cause the unstimulated auditory pathways to atrophy (reduce their functional activity). Research has shown that auditory stimulation and training will improve the auditory processing abilities of the individual; for example Jira in 1992 used an intervention programme which focused on intensive listening exercises. These emphasised auditory memory and language comprehension. At the end of the programme the children showed improvement on selected auditory tasks and both teachers and parents reported an improvement in overall school performance.

 Learning to play a musical instrument will help to improve auditory processing skills. Those students who are affected by both Dyspraxia and auditory processing difficulties may find it difficult to learn to play an instrument. *(For further information see 'Music Solutions No. 1 – Dyspraxia and learning to play a musical instrument' ISBN 1 901544 55 9.)*

Learning to play an instrument by ear (e.g. via the Suzuki method) can be beneficial to such students but they will take a long time to develop the skill and a good deal of patience and understanding is required of their music teachers and parents. Such students can take a very long time to go through the grades; e.g. five years to gain Grade 1 even for a very bright student. Towards the end of that time they may need to combine the strategies of both learning by ear and learning to read music. If the Suzuki method is adopted teachers and parents will need to ensure that the child does not feel out of place in the group lessons (which are part of such tuition) as their peers progress much faster than they do.

> What will work for one student will not work for another!

Bellis, in 'Assessment and Management of Central Auditory Processing Disorders in the Educational Setting' provides very good information on the management of auditory processing disorders. She recommends that intervention is multidisciplinary (e.g. involves professionals across a wide range of disciplines including teachers and speech and language therapists). Two of the key elements of intervention are that:

- The classroom environment be adapted to the student's difficulties so that little auditory effort is needed to learn academic tasks. The remediation environment however, should be gradually enriched with auditory information at a rate that is appropriate to the student's level of processing.

- The student's auditory difficulties are overcome by remediation activities and compensatory strategies. (An FM Radio Link system is very effective – either a personal one or with a speaker which gives consistent access to the speaker's/teacher's voice.) The student's Local Education Authority will have an Hearing Support Service which can advise on equipment, strategies etc. for students who have listening difficulties.

It is important to remember that each student will be different and each will have a different range of difficulties – what will work for one, will not work for another. Therefore, great care must be taken to suit the intervention programme to the particular student's needs. Intervention to help the child overcome their auditory difficulties should occur as soon as they are noticed. The 'Early Communication Skills' pack provides a wide range of activities (including auditory-based ones) that are designed to be carried out in the home environment for pre-school children under the supervision of a speech and language therapist.

Some schools use the 'ARROW' teaching method devised by Dr Colin Lane which is a useful auditory (listening) and writing-based teaching technique for spelling and reading where the student writes from his/her own pre-recorded dictation. (It does require specialist training from The ARROW Trust, Tel/Fax: 01278 441249, e-mail goarrow@self-voice.co.uk) ARROW has been shown to have very good results with most ages and poor writing ability does not seem to affect the results. Like all methods it is not suitable for everyone. Some students; e.g. those who are bright qualitative learners (having a grasshopper-type mind that dislikes having to do things in a particular order) and those who have Oppositional Defiant Disorder may find it difficult to accept learning by this means.

The 'Wordshark 2L' computer program is a useful auditory tool. The student's voice can be pre-recorded and heard whenever the word is on-screen. Clues to words can be given auditorally and visually. 'Auditory Processes' by P Gillet provides a huge number of simple strategies to overcome difficulties in each of the different auditory skills. Although it is aimed at classroom use many of the activities would also be suitable for home use. Care does, however, need to be taken that the activity chosen is appropriate to the student. Thus, in the auditory memory section the activity requiring the student to name objects in his/her environment may be too hard for some students with word finding/labelling difficulties. Listening skills can be improved through the use of the 'Listening Skills' books. Until phonological skills are improved, teaching via a phonological method is not going to be an efficient strategy. 'Sound Linkage' by P Hatcher provides auditory activities to improve phonological awareness as a way of overcoming reading difficulties. (Details of all these materials can be found in Appendix 5.)

1	2	3	4
5	6	7	8

Put the sheet on the table like this.

<u>Auditory closure activities</u> A useful strategy is to train the student to use contextual clues to work out what is likely to have been the missing word. It is best to use stories, poems etc. that s/he is familiar with to teach this skill and initially to miss out the final word of a line; e.g. Twinkle, twinkle little star, how I wonder what you ….

<u>Use of the Auditory Memory Enhancement strategy</u>
Divide a sheet of A4 blank paper into 8 boxes and number them. An adult reads text to the student. (Initially start by reading one paragraph at a time and each week add one more paragraph. Each page/paragraph should have at least one main concept.) After hearing the paragraph/s the student draws a sketch to show what it was about; e.g. the main concept. (Explain to him/her that s/he should draw stick men etc. as the sketches are not meant to look good; they are just meant to jog his/her memory when s/he tells the story at the end.) The adult should demonstrate the activity first.

The first sketch will be drawn in box number 1. After each sketch is drawn the next paragraph is read. Once the story is completed the student reviews the sketches and tells the story to the adult. Initially start with simple short stories, then gradually build up the activity so that a long story is told over several sessions. It is important to choose written material that is likely to be of interest to the student and if possible change the name of the main character to that of the student/include the student's pets etc. in the story. The adult could also use this activity to read sections of reference material relevant to current school projects.
<u>Week 1</u>: do the above activities four times a week. Days 1-2: allow 3 minutes for him/her to do the sketch. Days 3-4: allow 2 minutes for each sketch.
<u>Week 2 onwards</u>: do the activities 4 times a week. Allow 1 minute for each sketch.

Points to note: The time limit for the sketching is very important as it helps to develop many skills; e.g. memory access and recall skills, enables the student to make generalisations and also uses what has been called the 'visual-spatial sketch pad' subsystem of working memory. The sketch must show the main concept of the paragraph/section of text. If this does not occur then discussion, plus the adult re-reading the text and drawing a series of pictures to show each part of the story, will help the student to work out the main concept; e.g.

1. A tiger was asleep by a jungle path.　2. A little boy came along the jungle path.
3. The tiger woke up and attacked him.　4. Jane came along the path and heard a roar.
5. She rushed into the clearing.　6. She saw the tiger about to eat the little boy.
7. She shot the tiger & rescued the boy. 8. The boy was upset & she took him home.

The student could then be helped to work out which of the pictures would be necessary for someone to know what had happened by asking questions; e.g. Is the story all about a tiger that was asleep? Note: Sentence 7 tells us the main concept in the story.

<u>Strategies for making it easier for the student to understand instructions</u>
It is essential that student and teacher have a good relationship and are in harmony. The teacher will need to attract the student's attention before giving instructions. (This can be achieved by saying his/her name and then giving the instruction whilst physically demonstrating the task. This strategy may also help to reduce any word-finding/labelling difficulties that may be present. The teacher should ask the student to explain what s/he has to do before expecting him/her to do the task. Some students will only be able to remember the instruction if they draw a picture of/write down the task.

Chapter 6

SPECIFIC LANGUAGE IMPAIRMENT

Sections of this chapter have been contributed by AFASIC and edited by Jan Poustie. Further information on Language Impairments can be obtained from AFASIC – see Appendix 1.

TERMS USED TO DESCRIBE LANGUAGE DIFFICULTIES

Aphasia = no speech

Dysphasia = impaired speech

These are the oldest terms for describing speech and language difficulties. These Greek terms are usually used to describe acquired impairments of speech and language in adults. (This means that the impairments occurred after the person was born.) Children's difficulties are more usually described as expressive and receptive language difficulties.

Expressive difficulties	Receptive difficulties

Speaking & writing	**Listening & reading**
Difficulties in speaking (articulation) or using language. There can also be difficulties in using appropriate body language.	Problems in understanding the spoken or written word. There can also be difficulties in understanding other people's body language.

SPECIFIC LANGUAGE IMPAIRMENT CAUSES DIFFICULTIES IN:

- Word-finding (accessing words from memory)
- Word-labelling (remembering the names of objects etc.)
- Organising words into correct sentence order
- Organising one's thoughts
- Using grammar correctly
- Learning vocabulary
- Understanding humour
- Using higher level language (e.g. I 'ought to have' mowed the lawn.)
- Use of language
- Expressing what is known and understood (expressive language)
- Understanding what is heard or read (receptive language)
- Knowing which verb tense to use
- Use of prepositions (words that tell us the position of a thing in space; e.g. before)
- Understanding expressions such as 'cut it out', metaphors etc.
- Learning punctuation

Children with speech and language impairments have a range of difficulties. Some of these difficulties are obvious because the child has speech difficulties, and others are hidden because we have either not recognised the problem, or the child and the adults around the child have instinctively put in place strategies to accommodate their difficulties. Many children with Speech and Language impairments will also have a range of other difficulties which might include learning difficulties, motor problems, listening and attention difficulties, memory problems and organisational difficulties.

In recent years the relationship between spoken and written language has become increasingly clear, and we now recognise that development of speech and language skills is essential if literacy skills are to develop with any ease. The National Curriculum specifically identifies the need to develop the skills of reading, writing, spelling, speaking, listening and attention. Without these skills we can become isolated adults in society.

The word Dyslexia has become a familiar term used to describe difficulties with written language, and its relevance to speech and language impairments may not be immediately obvious. However, professionals are increasingly aware of the importance of developing speech and language skills **before** literacy skills and that particular speech impairments; e.g. phonological impairment etc., lead to difficulties with the acquisition of literacy skills.

Children in the early years need to develop:
- The ability to speak clearly
- The ability to articulate thoughts, requests and feelings
- Listening skills and attention skills.

The student's language difficulties may be hidden because we have not recognised them, or, because we have instinctively supported them.

With these skills in place they then need to move on to develop literacy-related skills:
- The knowledge of words and their meanings
- The development of concepts
- Awareness of pattern; e.g. clusters of sounds in words and rime. (Some people are not aware of the difference between the words 'rime' and 'rhyme'. Words rhyme when the end of them sounds the same; e.g. eight, late. Rime is when the final sound of two or more words both sound the same and contain the same letters. Thus thyme and time sound the same but they do not rime but time and slime do rime.)
- The ability to discriminate what they see and hear
- The ability to recognise words
- Memory skills and concentration skills
- An understanding of the order in which the events in a story occur
- An understanding of the language used in books. (Spoken language can be very different from written language. Written language is much more precise and flowing.)
- The language used to describe the different parts of a book; e.g. contents, index, title

All these skills need to be in place to enable a child to read and write with confidence.

Children with speech and language impairments, delays or disorders will almost certainly find their ability to read and write affected in some way. The following provides an overview of the range of difficulties that some children face.

EXPRESSIVE AND RECEPTIVE LANGUAGE
Most children with speech and language impairments will have difficulties in both areas, but will have a main difficulty in one area.

ARTICULATORY AND EXPRESSIVE DIFFICULTIES

- Verbal Dyspraxia (*see Chapter 4*)

- Phonological difficulties where the child has difficulty in pronouncing a number of sounds. The sounds which are mispronounced can be grouped according to certain features such as the place in the mouth where the sound is produced and how it is produced. The listener may not be able to understand the child's speech and this can lead to a great deal of frustration (for both the listener and the speaker). If this difficulty is present in the first child in the family the parents may not be aware that the child is trying to say words but other, more experienced parents, grandparents etc., may be able to recognise the words. The Edith Norrie Letter Case is a very useful tool for literacy for use by both teachers and speech and language therapists to improve articulation, phonological awareness and spelling and reading skills.

- Cluttering: where the child's speech can be so rapid and muddled that the listener cannot understand the child. (The speaker may be unconcerned, or unaware, of his/her difficulty.)

- Dysarthria: which affects speech production. The result is slurred speech due to weak, or incorrect, movements of the speech organs. Such difficulties can range from mild to severe and in most cases the speech is slow and limited in range. Again, due to articulatory difficulties, many of these children have difficulties in acquiring literacy skills.

Students with articulatory difficulties can benefit from using the Tok apparatus which enables them to hear their own voice more clearly. (Normally we mainly 'hear' what we say through the vibrations which are conducted through our ear bones. This apparatus enables students to hear via the vibrations through the air.) Alternatively, students can hear their own voice more clearly if they put their hands over their ears.

RECEPTIVE, OR COMPREHENSION, DIFFICULTIES

This is where the child's ability to understand spoken and written language is impaired. For these children it is important to consider listening and speaking skills separately, as the two will not be working together effectively. Language comprehension is the understanding of what words and phrases mean in sentences. It involves:

1 Hearing
2 Paying attention to the sounds in speech (the presence of Attention Deficits can affect this)
3 Distinguishing (or discriminating between speech sounds). This is known as Auditory Discrimination
4 The ability to process language
5 The ability to remember the sequence of sounds (this is known as Auditory Sequential Memory)
6 Knowing word meanings (semantics)
7 Understanding sentence structure (grammar)
8 Making sense of language in and out of context
9 Seeing clearly the text
10 Knowing how, and when, to question the information read or listened to.

The presence of Central Auditory Processing Disorder can affect 1, 2, 3, 4.

Difficulties in understanding the speech of the child can cause great distress and frustration to both the child and the listener.

Breakdown in any, or a number, of these areas will affect the child's ability to understand and will impair his/her ability to interact with (and understand) the world s/he lives in. His/her ability to read and write will be affected in a number of ways and there may be difficulties in accessing the National Curriculum.

If receptive language difficulties (e.g. slow auditory processing and reduced short-term memory difficulties and/or Central Auditory Processing Disorder are present then the speaker may become frustrated with the listener. The listener may be accused of:

- Not paying attention
- Misbehaving
- Giving up trying
- Doing the exact opposite of what s/he was told to do
- Being slow to carry out the instruction
- Carrying out the instruction incorrectly (or not carrying it out at all!).

There are materials available that help with such difficulties one of which is Listening Skills (see Appendix 5).

Language difficulties cause problems when writing creatively, or factually.

Auditory sequential memory

This is the ability to hear a sequence of sounds, words or sentences, and be able to hold them in memory for sufficient time as to be able to:

- gain information from them
- process and organise that information
- respond to that information.

Many children with a history of late speaking and early speech and language difficulties find that, although these difficulties resolve, there are residual problems (problems that are still present) that only parents and teachers can detect. The key factor in this is limited auditory sequential memory span which is apparent in the child's difficulties with reading and writing. By the time that the student has reached secondary age, it is unlikely that the memory span will improve significantly. However, auditory memory training activities/ strategies combined with teaching the student to use a multisensory approach which favours his/her natural learning style can improve the student's ability to function in the classroom.

Memory difficulties can often be mistaken for laziness and it is important that both the child and those around him/her are aware of the problem and that strategies to address the problem are in place; e.g.

- Train the student to cluster (group) information so instead of learning the telephone number 289559 as 'two - eight - nine - five - five - nine' the student remembers it as 'twenty-eight, ninety-five, fifty-nine' or as two groups of three digits – 289, 559.

- Using auditory games to train the student to remember a longer string of items. Thus, the tutor and the student can take turns to add one more item to a list with each person having to say the whole list before they add their item on to it; e.g.
⇒ I went down the High Street and bought a Gameboy
⇒ I went down the High Street and bought a Gameboy and a large ice cream.

- Using auditory games to train the student to remember events. Thus the tutor and the student can take turns to add one more event, action, person, description etc. with the items that are added being included at any part of the story; e.g.
⇒ On Saturday I went swimming
⇒ On Saturday morning I went swimming

⇒ On Saturday morning I went swimming in the sea.

- Using electronic apparatus to improve the student's ability to integrate visual, auditory and kinaesthetic (movement) memory. Two particularly useful tools – 'Miniwizard' and 'Simon' do not appear to be available commercially any more but they can be found in jumble and car boot sales.

- Do not talk for too long and do not assume that everything that you have said has been processed/understood/heard.

- Provide visual memory hooks for the information that you are presenting; e.g. single words in different colours on the board, or better still pictures, BUT allow the student to look at the word/picture and process the information from it before you carry on talking.

Jason

Always check that the student is listening and has focused his attention on you before giving verbal information. You can do this by saying the student's name and gaining eye contact.

A variety of materials exist to help with the development of receptive language skills but it really is a case of what will suit one student will not suit another. LDA stock a range of materials which can help develop particular listening and reading skills; e.g. ' Listen and Do' and boxes of 'Reading for Comprehension' cards. The latter focus on different aspects of comprehension e.g. inferences and deduction but they may not be suitable for those with moderate to severe Dyslexia. When Attention Deficits are present students are likely to need materials designed for them personally that relate to their family/interests as otherwise they will be bored by the materials and will not learn the skills. There is a great shortage of materials suitable for the older student and this unfortunately means that tutors need to find the time to make their own resources – something which in a busy working and home life is not always easy to achieve.

SEMANTIC-PRAGMATIC DISORDER

'Semantics' is the meaning of words and 'pragmatics' is the social use of language. Some students who have difficulties in these areas will appear to have good mechanical reading skills. They may have age appropriate grammatical skills and 'on the surface' may appear to use appropriate language. Although some might demonstrate mild verbal (articulatory) Dyspraxia, most have fluent speech. However, closer examination of their understanding shows that they have particular difficulties with the conceptual aspects of language, particularly with regard to the language relating to 'time' (temporal) and that relating to 'space', i.e. location (spatial). These students may be unaware of categorisation – for example, that knives and forks are 'cutlery'. There can be a failure to understand language associated with a topic e.g. weather, because the student can understand information at a basic level and label things; e.g. 'sun', but explaining 'sunshine' is another matter altogether. The same can occur when looking at an apple tree for when there are no apples on it the student may not accept that it can be an apple tree! These students tend to take language at a literal level and do not understand meaning which is embedded (found within) either text, or spoken language. Examples of embedded language are:

- Metaphor; e.g. when instead of saying that someone is as fierce as a tiger the word 'tiger' is used to refer to the person – "the grey-haired tiger ruled his children".
- Irony – here the person is saying the opposite of what he means.
- Sarcasm

41

When mixing with others these students often do not know how to start or maintain a conversation. Their social skills, body language and facial expression may be impaired and they may fail to recognise these signals in others. When Attention Deficits are present students may need to be taught some of these skills too; e.g. understanding body language. These skills have to be taught by strategies such as:

- Modelling body language – the tutor shows the student how the face looks when s/he is angry, slightly annoyed, worried, sad, happy etc. and the student with the help of a mirror creates the same face. Then the tutor and the student take turns to model the face whilst the other person guesses the emotion. However, such students do need to be able to recognise the emotion within themselves first and so the tutor should discuss prior to the modelling how one feels when one is angry, happy etc. Specialist intervention, e.g. from a speech and language therapist, is likely to be needed if the student is unable to recognise his/her own emotions. It is absolutely essential that children from as young an age as possible (e.g. pre-school) are taught these skills. If this does not occur it can appear to the child that adults suddenly 'lose their tempers' without warning. Such children do not recognise the facial and body signs of the adult slowly losing patience with the child. This can make the student feel very insecure especially in the school environment. An American computer programme called 'Gaining Face' might be of use here as it has been designed to teach students facial expressions (see http://www.ccoder.com/GainingFace for further information).
- Role plays of social situations.
- Use of materials such as SULP (Social Use of Language Programme by Wendy Rinaldi, secondary school version from NFER-Nelson Tel: 01753 858961, primary school version from Child Communication and Learning Tel: 01483 458411).

A student may have semantic difficulties without pragmatic problems; however a student with pragmatic problems will always have semantic difficulties. This latter group may be viewed by some professionals as being within the autistic spectrum, although they may not merit a diagnosis of autism. However, there is still much academic debate concerning this matter.

Higher Level Language Impairment (HLL)
This book has already discussed the 'grey area' between the behavioural conditions (Dyspraxia, Autistic Spectrum Disorder and Attention Deficits). The existence of Higher Level Language Impairment appears to be another 'grey area'.

Such students can appear to be complete contradictions – at one moment there can appear to be little wrong with their use of (and understanding of language); the next moment there can be a lack of comprehension or totally inappropriate use of language. Difficulties that can be seen include:

Limited social development may be apparent when Higher Level Language Disorder is present.

- Taking turns during conversation
- Keeping the conversation flowing and/or being unclear about what they are saying. (This may be partly due to word finding and word labelling difficulties and difficulties with the organisation of language)
- Some of the behaviours associated with Autistic Spectrum Disorder may be apparent; e.g. like their room set out in a certain way, idiosyncratic behaviours and limited interests.

Such students may find the transition between one type of provision and another difficult. Thus the transition from playgroup to school may be difficult though the difficulties are likely to be more obvious when in transition from infant to junior and then again when the child enters secondary school. The infant/junior transition is made more difficult because the infant curriculum is usually fairly concrete (lots of handing of objects in order to learn concepts and processes). Therefore, HLL does not start to show significantly (to the uninitiated) until top infants. The difficulties in transition from playgroup to primary school can be present because such children:

- Can no longer base their interactions with other children on physical play and physical activities
- No longer have a high ratio of adults/pupils within their environment and so do not have an adult 'at hand' to help them socialise and relate to others. This ratio of staff to children is a major problem when our children are entering school at four years of age rather than attending a pre-school establishment.
- Once they attend school they also have less time to play with objects/toy people which enable them to model and role play situations. Such activities can be very important to this group as they may not be able to explain their problem (nor understand it themselves). The modelling and role playing with objects and toys also enable such students to communicate their worries etc. to the adults around them.

All students who have Asperger Syndrome also have Higher Level Language Impairment.

Both professionals and parents can miss the signs of language difficulties in students, especially when the student is of above average, or high intelligence, as their intellectual ability can mask the condition.

Some parents assume that the child who can make their views known at home but who talks little in the classroom and other social settings is just 'shy'. Sometimes teachers do not make the connection between advanced reading skills (or oral work) and written work that is of a lower standard. It is also easy for teachers to underestimate such students and their abilities. Educational psychologists, too, may not see the warning signs of the presence of a language impairment. One sign is when a student who has good to excellent written comprehension skills performs poorly during the aural (listening) comprehension tasks within an assessment of intellectual ability; e.g. a WISC or BAS assessment. Such a situation can occur when there are language and/or auditory processing difficulties.

It is generally recognised that when Dyspraxia, Dyslexia and Dyscalculia are present there is also likely to be a language impairment of some type which will vary in severity from mild to severe and with either, or both, expressive and receptive language being affected. Sometimes one of the parents of the student also has a language impairment too. Parents may often feel very concerned that their child will fail to achieve qualifications and will fail to cope in social situations etc.

When Specific Language Impairment is present the child is at risk of having a very unhappy time at school (both within the classroom and in the playground) with the situation being far

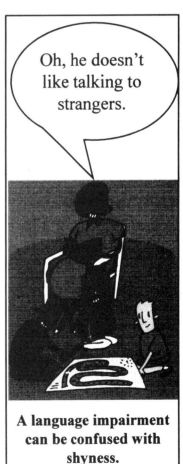

Oh, he doesn't like talking to strangers.

A language impairment can be confused with shyness.

worse if their problems are undiagnosed and unprovided for. (Such problems may carry on into adulthood with the adult having only a very small circle of social contacts.) Even those who are highly intelligent can be badly affected in the school situation if they are not supported, as the following case studies show. However, some of these cases also show that such students (when supported) can achieve a great deal and our expectation should be that we will enable them to achieve their potential rather than see their language difficulties limiting them throughout their lives.

Case Study 1 – Child A

Language Impairment may cause even highly intelligent students to be forced into unusual behaviours. The less supported the child, the more stress she will be under and so there are more likely to be such behaviours. One such pupil happily attended a pre-school playgroup and a nursery. However, she would hide under the dining-room table and refuse to get dressed prior to going to school in the morning. She would then spend part of the school day sitting in a corner of the reception classroom with her thumb in her mouth. Her teacher failed to recognise that this child was in distress. The child's behaviours occurred because both her academic and social needs were not being met, with the school failing to recognise that they had a highly intelligent pupil who could already read before she attended school.

This child's situation could have been markedly improved if the school had accepted the information on the child's skills which had been provided by her pre-school playgroup and her mother. Instead they relied on a test administered by the school during the girl's first term which was designed to find out whether the child was ready to read. As this test showed that the child was **not** 'ready to read' the fact that she could already do so was ignored!!

(Even with the assessment of pupils upon entry to the reception class that now occurs in state schools, liaison between pre-school groups and the child's school must be more than just a visit to the group by the reception teacher. Pre-school playgroup leaders and nursery staff are professionals and should be regarded as such. Their input to health visitors and teachers can be invaluable and if they indicate concerns regarding a child's functioning, or state that the child has achieved 'such and such' a skill level, then they should be believed. If, once the child enters the school, that skill level is not apparent then that in itself is cause for concern as it is an indicator that the child is not functioning appropriately in the school environment.)

In Child A's case the transition between playgroup/nursery and school had been slightly eased because the school had a policy of children attending for only part of the day for the first part of the reception term. However, although the mother realised that the child was not thriving in the school setting the school did not. Teachers may see a child that 'clings' and is then 'perfectly happy during the day', or see a child who leaves his/her mother with no hesitation and then shows no obvious signs of distress. Children, like adults, learn to mask their feelings and some learn this very early for fear of being teased by their peer group or, in unfortunate cases, by the adults around them. Just as an adult would not show his distress whilst in the company of non-family members these children do not show their distress by crying, or by being angry. Instead they may become very passive and insecure, may misbehave, or have far more illnesses, because of the stress that they are under. There may

  **Times of transition (e.g. moving house, changing schools, classes) can be a problem for children affected by language impairment.**

also be a noticeable change in behaviour between holidays/weekends and during the school term. After a long period in school (e.g. by Year 4 and above) there may be little difference between school and non-school behaviour as by that time the child is under so much stress that she cannot 'unwind' even during the long summer holiday. Child A found the transition from primary school to secondary school equally difficult and actually became hysterical during her second week of secondary school and refused to attend. It took a great deal of persuasion on the part of the mother plus a flexible attitude on the part of the school (in allowing the child to attend for just a lesson a day for a short while) to solve this problem.

More than one condition can be present so when Language Impairment is present we may also see other conditions within the SpLD Profile. This particular student had noticeable receptive language difficulties and Articulatory Dyspraxia, Dyscalculia and phonological difficulties (which are commonly associated with the presence of Dyslexia) were also present. However, her difficulties in learning to read would not have been apparent to most teachers and parents and so they would have failed to recognise them. This was especially the case with regard to this student as she, by the age of five years, was already reading with total comprehension and accuracy at 150 wpm (words per minute).

Child A was totally unable to learn to read words phonologically and learnt purely by visual methods. The reading scheme used by her school contained a small amount of phonic work which totally confused her and it was agreed with the school that she would not be asked to do such work. (This child would have found the present Literacy Hour activities equally confusing. She would also have found its phonological activities slow and frustrating, especially as her visual memory skills were so advanced that she could learn new words at speed.) Once she had seen a word five times she had learnt it but each ending added to the word meant that it was a completely new word to her. Thus she learnt 'sleep', 'sleeping' and 'sleeps' as totally separate visual images. It was only because she had an excellent visual memory and was very intelligent that she was able to achieve this.

It was not until she had a reading age of 8+ years that she was able to learn a few 'sound patterns'. Later she was taught how to recognise the syllables in words by placing the flat of her hand under her chin (which works for most words if words are said clearly). By the age of fourteen years she was able to read at 1400 wpm with almost perfect comprehension. Her practice of repeatedly re-reading her favourite books had enabled her to gain this speed and it is a very useful strategy for those affected by literacy difficulties. Her receptive language difficulties were overcome, to a large extent, by her receiving specialist music tuition from the age of five. First she learnt to play an instrument via the Suzuki method which traditionally concentrates on auditory skills. Then she joined a music appreciation class where she learnt the recorder and was introduced to the reading of music via a recorder book in which the notes were colour coded. Later she joined school choirs and a strings orchestra.

By the age of eleven years Child A gained a SAT Level 6 (only 2% of the population gain such a high level and this puts her into the gifted/superior intellectual ability category). She

Counting syllables

Some people teach students to count syllables by clapping as they hear them in the word. A more reliable method is to do the following:
- Make the hand flat. Place it in a horizontal position palm downwards
- Put the hand so that it is just below (and touching) the chin.
- Keep the hand in place and say the word; e.g. 'hundred'
- Count 1 syllable every time the hand moves down.

 **Some children with language impairment will not be able to cope with highly complex language such as Shakespeare. Others will be able to cope, to various degrees, as long as we provide them with plenty of support and introduce them to difficult language in very small stages and in enjoyable ways.**

was now able to understand and enjoy the Shakespeare cartoon videos. (These are an excellent introduction to Shakespeare as the highly visual content enables the language to be understood.) At twelve years she was able to regard her first visit to the Royal Shakespeare Company's production of The Merry Wives of Windsor as 'fabulous'. (Comedies are a good introduction to Shakespeare as the large amount of action within the play helps the student to understand the language.) At fourteen years she was able to cope with tragedy too, though she was still finding it a little difficult to focus on the language for the whole length of the play.

At age fifteen this student still frequently mispronounces words (usually by putting the wrong emphasis on a word, not knowing unusual sound patterns; e.g. 'tian' or by not knowing whether the vowel sound is long (e.g. 'a' as in 'cape') or short (e.g. 'a' as in 'cap'). It took a long time for her to learn to use the correct tenses and there are still errors of this type in both her written and oral language. Proverbs and metaphors were particularly difficult for her to understand but once understood she was able to use the latter in her written work with good effect. Her spelling is very good as she has developed a highly effective, totally visual, strategy for remembering the letter patterns. She still finds some social situations difficult. Understanding the expectations of the different teachers at secondary school and when 'rules can be bent' has been difficult for her to learn and she still can find 'handling' people of her own age 'tricky', especially when they are not close friends. She is very imaginative and writes very good short stories and poems.

Case Study 2 – Child B

It can seem rather surprising to both parents and teachers that a person who has a language impairment can function well in a theatre environment. Sometimes, if Dyspraxia is present, such students may move with a certain lack of grace but apart from that (and possible problems in picking up the social cues of others) their acting can be very good. Even students with considerable expressive language difficulties can enjoy and produce good performances simply because they do not have to think about the words they speak. Acting does not require the student to work out the construction of the sentence, work out what he wants to say and make sure that the verb tenses, prepositions etc. are correct.

Thus the mother of this young man and his teachers were misled by the student's apparent language skills in drama and his functioning at GCSE level. He was criticised for his lack of contribution to classroom discussion and outside of school his mother just thought that he was 'shy' with strangers. The mother had instinctively put in support strategies for the student. Consequently, his underlying problems with language were not identified until the age of seventeen when he was having great problems with coping with his 'A' level studies and was in great distress. Even then his special needs were not apparent to his teachers although his mother had realised that 'something was wrong' though she did not know what the problem was. He often used his mother as a 'translator' for both oral and written language and became increasingly under stress as he progressed through secondary school. His planning and organisational skills were very weak, his handwriting was poor (Graphomotor Dyspraxia was the main cause of this) and he was being criticised for failing to produce work and being lazy. His problems were considerable but no-one had recognised them for what they were because his determination, motivation and high intelligence masked his difficulties.

Case Study 3 – Girl B

This student had severe expressive and receptive language difficulties as did her mother. Her brother was also affected by expressive written language difficulties. Girl B's receptive language difficulties were so severe that she had difficulties in understanding the teacher and so tended to switch off. Her language difficulties resulted in her having virtually no friends at school, being unable to read more than a few words and being unable to express her thoughts either orally or in writing. Her difficulties were also affecting her acquisition of mathematical skills. She started to receive specialist support from the author when she was seven years old. Within two terms she was able to function within the classroom and had a group of school friends. Within five terms she was able to speak and (with support) write good quality sentences and, although she was still an inaccurate reader, she found great pleasure in reading (with support) Winnie the Pooh.

BULLYING

Language impairments can make a student more vulnerable, especially when they are present alongside another condition which can cause the student to have problems in interacting/ playing with others (e.g. Dyspraxia, Attention Deficits, Autistic Spectrum Disorder, etc.) or causes them to have low self-esteem because they do not obtain good grades in their work no matter how hard they try. This vulnerability makes them an easy target for being bullied by their peer group physically or verbally. Verbal bullying by members of their family and even in some cases by their teachers can also occur.

Some professionals can also be responsible for verbally bullying the parent. It is often the mother who does most of the communicating with the school. She is very vulnerable to being bullied especially if she lacks good language skills herself and/or has low self-esteem. She may be at her 'wits end' because she does not know how to communicate her great concerns for her child and explain the problems that the child is experiencing. Fathers too can find it difficult to explain their concerns, especially as unlike most women a number of men prefer 'action rather than words' and find discussion difficult. (One of the parents may just 'hide' from the problems by believing that if they ignore them then they will just go away.) Unless the child is at boarding school s/he will spend more time with his/her family than at school. If the teacher, or other professional, is finding it difficult/stressful to cope with the situation and to find solutions for the child's problems then how much more stressful is the parent's situation? We cannot support the child effectively if we do not support the parents. This means that we must communicate and liase with the parents on a regular basis and regard them as being part of a true partnership rather than just a token one that can occur in some educational establishments.

Many children with speech and language difficulties will experience problems with the acquisition of literacy skills. For some of them this will be a result of their speech and language impairment, for others Dyslexia will be an additional difficulty over and above their speech and language difficulty.

 **If one of the parents has a language difficulty then professionals must take great care to ensure that information is understood and that the parent is enabled to put his/her point of view across.**

LANGUAGE SKILLS ARE VITAL – WE CANNOT IGNORE THEM!!

Language difficulties create a vicious circle.

- In order to process information we need to think.
- In order to think we use language.
- In order to communicate our thoughts we need to use oral or written language.
- In order to understand those around us, and to learn information, we need to be able to process the language that we hear and read.
- In order to learn language and thus gain a good command of it (e.g. grammar, vocabulary etc.) we need to speak it, and hear it and later on to write it and read it.
- If we cannot speak, hear (and process) language to a standard appropriate to our age and intellectual ability then we have less language skills than our peers. Consequently, our language difficulties will cause us to have problems in processing information when we think, write, speak, hear or read and so on ... and so on ...

The only way that those affected by these problems can break out of this vicious circle is for us to enable them to overcome their difficulties and support them so that they can succeed in their academic and life goals. Such individuals require:

1   Early identification
2   Specific targeted provision through speech and language programmes
3   Appropriate multisensory teaching that targets their natural learning style
4   Specialist teaching, and speech and language therapy.
5   Effective liaison between the various professionals involved with the student; and liaison between the professionals, the parents and the student.

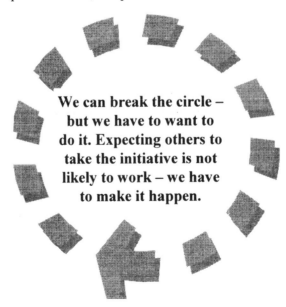

We can break the circle – but we have to want to do it. Expecting others to take the initiative is not likely to work – we have to make it happen.

Chapter 7

Vision problems – their effects on learning, and how to help, both at home and in the classroom

By Keith Holland B.Sc., FCOptom., FCOVD, FAAO, DCLP and edited by Jan Poustie

PART 1
Based upon an original article by Keith C Holland.

The visual demands of reading, writing and education are very complex, and naturally stressful to the human body. The way in which we adapt to, and cope with, them will affect our whole approach to learning and in many cases shape our personality for the future. This chapter sets out to provide a framework for the teacher and interested parent to:

- understand something of the difficulties that can occur
- provide guidance on how to recognise and manage such difficulties
- provide information on what can be done within a classroom setting to help – both by improving visual functioning and by direct training.

ACUITY

When we consider sight, the first and most obvious concern is whether or not an individual is able to see well. This skill is known as **acuity,** and is the subject of the all too familiar letter-chart test carried out in school medicals, sight tests – and indeed just about

In every classroom in the land, in every group of student – quite possibly in every home of every reader of this chapter, there are children who are underachieving due to visual difficulties.

They may be able to 'see' well, they may have healthy eyes, but the tasks we take for granted of reading, writing and spelling are for them:
- harder work
- require greater effort
- less rewarding
- possibly almost impossible to satisfactorily complete.

every time that eyes are looked at. But this test is limited in its usefulness. It only provides basic information as to whether the person is able to see detail clearly; e.g. letters, the elements of shapes etc. It will not provide any information as to whether:
- the person can do this effortlessly
- discomfort occurs
- the same skill transfers to close work.

To look at these areas, other skills must be investigated.

CLOSE WORK

This involves three primary visual skills, each of which must function efficiently in its own right and yet also work together well (integrate) with the other two skills. This integration is itself a function of still other skills, and integration itself may be affected by stress.

The visual system is unique – no other body sensory system:
- is as complex
- has such complex interactions with other areas (an interaction is where one or more elements of a thing have an effect upon each other)
- relies so much upon extrinsic stress factors.

In order to have a functioning visual system three areas need to be considered:

A cornerstone is the stone at the top of an arch – if this stone is not present the arch will fall down. Effortless visual function is fundamental to learning, and is the cornerstone of how we acquire information about the world around us.

Focusing

How the person makes an object in space the clearest and most central object in their space world. This is controlled by the flexing of a small lens located inside the eyeball itself which is controlled by a series of small muscles, known as the ciliary muscles. In turn, these muscles are controlled by nerves, both of a voluntary nature and of an involuntary nature. (Voluntary muscles can be controlled by the person; e.g. we use muscles to move our head. Involuntary muscles cannot be controlled by the person; e.g. muscles within the gut move our food/waste material through our body.) Whilst this may seem to be of technical interest only, the effect of this involuntary control is crucial and will be looked at later.

Convergence

How the person teams their eyes together in order to ensure a co-ordinated, three dimensional (ideally) and stable image that can be seen long enough to trigger a meaningful mental representation so that cognition (understanding) can occur. Each eyeball is moved by six muscles, up, down, left, right, and in a rotary fashion. Control of these is very complex, with breakdown leading to double vision, confusion and, where it occurs early in life, a squint. Fortunately, we have very good devices that help us to overcome such problems and to cope with breakdown so that symptoms are kept to a minimum. However, there will always be a loss of depth perception and efficiency when the two eyes fail to work together properly.

Tracking – or eye movement skills

This term describes the skills needed to maintain fixation on (stay looking at) a moving object, or alternatively, the ability to select an object that we wish to look at and so move our attention from one object in our visual world to another. Whilst the same muscles that move the eyes are involved, they must integrate (combine) with focus in order to ensure that what we want to look at is kept right in the centre of our field of attention. This same integration is needed to ensure that if the object moves, then the eyes move by just the right amount to maintain fixation.

You can see the effects of tracking breakdown by trying to follow your own finger as you move it from side to side about twelve inches away from the nose. As the finger is moved faster and faster a point is reached where you can no longer see the finger clearly. At this point you will usually start to become more aware of what is behind the finger in the background.

There are two further aspects of vision that need to be considered. Firstly, the size of the area that can be concentrated upon and the impact that stress has on this. Secondly, the speed at which information can be assimilated (taken in) visually.

1. THE VISUAL AREA

A child who can see and take in ten syllables at once on a page will be at an obvious advantage over one who can only see five. Furthermore, the smaller the area of detailed visual attention, the more likely it is that the individual will be distracted by information that is not required for the task coming from the periphery. (The periphery is the area surrounding the bit that you want to look at.) This is of particular relevance in cases of ADHD and Dyspraxia, where peripheral distraction can be a major negative influence to learning.

Visual stress

This is a critical factor to consider. An individual under stress will stimulate what is known as their 'Sympathetic Nervous System' - nicknamed the 'fight and flight' system. The purpose of this system is to take over body control in emergencies, and this occurs through the release of a chemical into the bloodstream known as adrenaline. Now adrenaline disturbs the normal relationships between focusing and convergence, leading to greater effort being needed when looking at objects near to you in order to maintain focus; e.g. when reading. In turn, this lowers cognition, or thinking, and can rapidly lead to fatigue and concentration loss. Some research studies have suggested that this visual stress response is one of the most common causes of reduced abilities when working. Fortunately, correction of this is usually comparatively easy with appropriate lenses, although the testing required to identify this is far from being widespread at this time in Britain.

2. SPEED OF INFORMATION PROCESSING

The **speed of information processing** is vital to ensure fast cognition. Where speed is slow,

Our fight or flight system is stimulated by stress.
Stress causes the body to release adrenaline and it:
- Makes it more difficult for the person to maintain focus; e.g. on reading/writing tasks
- Lowers understanding of the material being read/our ability to think
- Increases tiredness
- Reduces concentration.

the stimulus (item that the person is looking at; e.g. a word/letter etc.) may have passed before cognition has occurred. This leads to wasted opportunities, boredom and attention loss. It has been suggested that in two individuals where all other factors are equal, the child who processes faster will be the more 'intelligent'.

Visual imagery skills

People who have a history of visual information-processing difficulties are quite probably going to exhibit poor visual imagery skills. In other words they will tend to think in non visual ways – probably using auditory and verbal clues and memories. Whilst this can be useful, it is naturally less efficient than the use of visual information, and can greatly slow down the whole process of learning and thinking. The person who can mentally recall the appearance of a word will find it much easier not only to spell the word but also to recognise when it is misspelled than will the subject who has to rely on an auditory word pattern. Visual memory is known as a simultaneous, or global skill, whilst auditory/verbal memory is essentially successive, or sequential, in nature.

It is only when all the above-mentioned skills operate together in an effortless and stress-free manner that optimal cognition and information processing can occur. It is important to recognise, however, that even in less than perfect situations, the miracle of learning can and will still occur, although at a lesser level.

> **"If we want to understand the child, we must understand how they learn; if we want to understand how they learn, we must understand their vision." (A. Gessel 1942).**

RECOGNISING THE PROBLEMS

The signs of visual difficulties are really quite simple to spot, and the use of a standardised questionnaire can make this quite easy. The questionnaire found in Appendix 4 has been used by Keith Holland for many years, and is only one of many such designs available that have been in use over the last fifty years.

If we do not ask the right questions then we cannot find out whether visual difficulties are present. Unrecognised visual difficulties can lead the child to believe that s/he is 'thick' and parents/teachers may believe that s/he is lazy.

GUIDE TO USING THE QUESTIONNAIRE FOUND IN APPENDIX 4

Two important things to recognise when using any questionnaire are that symptoms will change with time and with fatigue (tiredness), and that the child may not in fact report symptoms unless s/he is asked directly. Many children (who have never previously complained of any visual symptoms) when asked if print goes double, or moves about, whilst reading report that "Oh yes, it does, but then doesn't it do so for everyone?" This occurs often to the horror of their parents, who have assumed that silence in this area means absence of difficulty! The child's perspective is that they are somehow 'thick' for not being able to cope with what they assume others find it easy to deal with.

This notion that children have (of their inferiority in coping with what they assume others deal with) goes well beyond the realms of vision. It is often a key factor with children who are teased, or who perceive themselves as failing, and they will often have very negative self-images. Their self-image can be unwittingly reinforced by parents and teachers if they constantly emphasise the difficulties, and fail to spot and to highlight the child's strengths and successes, which may well be far greater than the difficulties. Adults may also fail to talk with the child about their own difficulties, leaving the child to feel inferior to the parent/ teacher etc., and somehow not living up to the expectations and ideals which s/he perceives has been set for him/her.

When looking for signs of potential visual difficulties, bear in mind that symptoms will usually be reduced – or even absent during holiday time, and may take a while to reappear at the start of term again. Visual difficulties are very much a factor of stress and fatigue, and may become worse during exams, or when other factors (possible home difficulties for example) are increased. The child who starts off reading fairly fluently, but whose performance deteriorates after a few lines, or when in the 'body' of a large paragraph, is a definite candidate for further checking.

 **Parents and teachers may have specific learning difficulties too. They can help the child develop a better self-image by explaining their own problems and the strategies that they use to overcome them.**

Visual skills affect handwriting
Many factors apart from vision can contribute to writing difficulty –
it is after all one of the most complex hand/eye tasks that the human
is capable of mastering. Poor visual motor skills can have a
significant effect upon writing, and correction with appropriate
means can have a real, and beneficial, effect upon it.

Visual problems can have differing effects on children, depending on the:
- duration of the problem
- severity of the problem
- personality of the child.

An additional factor may also be the effect of external stress – for example the expectations and demands placed on the child by parents, or by school.

THE EFFECTS OF VISUAL PROBLEMS ON VISUAL IMAGERY DEVELOPMENT

Visual problems can affect visual imagery development, which in turn can affect learning style.

- The non-imager will tend not to absorb information presented visually, or at least will tend not to take in visual detail.

- Unless the material has also been presented aurally (by something they listen to), or in some animated form (e.g. on television, or in a film), they may skim over the material in order to acquire highlights, but it will be without depth.

- Spelling will tend to be very erratic, with inconsistent errors – simply because the child does not recognise that they are spelling differently on one line to another! This can often lead to complaints of 'carelessness' by teachers if they are unaware of this type of problem.

- Poor imagery can also affect spatial development and hinder the development of concepts in, for example, mathematics.

- A child who cannot visualise space and volume is likely to have difficulty understanding number concepts in concrete terms, and may only 'succeed' in maths by slavishly following learned formulae and techniques, but without a real grasp of the effects that the formulae can have on the numbers themselves.

STRATEGIES THAT CAN HELP

The parent and teacher of a child with visual difficulties should consider the home/school environment for work, and ensure that it is optimised wherever possible. A few simple rules to follow include:

1   Make sure that the work surface is at an appropriate height to the child.
   • Ideally when sitting in an upright position, the elbows should just touch the desk when the arms are downward. This should ensure the desk is around fourteen inches lower than the eyes.
   • A slightly sloping desk helps to ensure that the head does not tip too far forwards – even the simple strategy of placing a ring binder underneath a book so that it tips slightly forward can help.

2   The eyes should keep at least twelve inches away from the text at all times.
   • The optimum (best) working distance from eye to page has been shown to equal the distance from the middle knuckle to the elbow in an outstretched hand.

If working at a desk, a small angle-poise type of light can be useful as this can easily be directed where needed.	

3   Ensure good, even light that is shadow-free, yet is not glaring.
     • Always work with good background light, and not just with the desk light on in an otherwise darkened room.
     • Try not to work under fluorescent lighting – including the so-called 'energy-saver' bulbs.
     • Good daylight is ideal, but can easily produce glare.
4   Take frequent visual breaks. Try to stop working for at least five minutes every thirty, and, in between times, frequently look up and around the room to break the stare that can so easily develop when concentrating.

WITHIN THE CLASSROOM THERE ARE A NUMBER OF KEY POINTS TO CONSIDER

Position in the class
•   Children with short-term memory problems in particular can find copying almost impossible if they have first to locate where the board is behind them before they even begin to copy!
•   The child with visual difficulties is probably best placed somewhere in the centre of the front third of the class, neither too close to, nor too far from, the board (when used).
•   It is essential that they do not have to look around in order to copy from a board, and can simply look up and down!

Space
Today's modern classroom may well be overcrowded, with a number of children sharing a desk or table. Whilst this may be useful for the development of social skills, it can cause difficulty for a child who is readily distracted by movement in their periphery.
•   Such children really need to be accommodated on their own desk, with sufficient space around them to provide a stable and static environment without extraneous (extra movements) to distract.
•   The desk, of course, should ideally be angled at about twenty degrees to optimise postural demands.

Time
Given the poor visual concentration that may be exhibited, work may need to be kept in 'bite-sized chunks' of around fifteen minutes to ensure high level concentration. Tony Buzan (in his book 'Use your Head') explains that long before symptoms arise, the child with difficulties may only be working at around fifty per cent of their capability. It makes sense therefore to stop well before this point for a short break, preferably involving movement and a change of visual activity. (Ways of reducing the written element of tasks are explored in 'Planning and Organisation Solutions' and 'Successful Strategies' both by Jan Poustie. See Appendix 5 for details.)

Concrete aids help with mathematics
Children with visual imagery difficulties may benefit from increased use of concrete aids when working to help develop an understanding of size, volume and space, and the effects of operations such as adding, subtracting, multiplying and dividing upon these. The need for such aids may extend well past the time that other children can do without them. (For more information on this topic, see 'Mathematics for Dyslexia' by Chinn and Ashcroft ISBN 1 86156 043 5, published by Whurr Books and 'Mathematics Solutions – An introduction to Dyscalculia' by Jan Poustie et al (ISBN 1 901544 20 6 published by Next Generation).

The personality continuum

There tend to be two 'types' of personality seen in children, but the reader should consider these as two ends of a continuum with a child being at some point on that line.

Type A─────────────────────────**Type B**

From a visual point of view, either approach can lead to changes in the visual system – 'Function alters structure'!

Both types of individuals may have difficulties with spatial skills, affecting sport and distance judgement, particularly in badminton and small ball games such as tennis, badminton, rounders and cricket. Typically however, they may not show difficulty in sports such as football and rugby where the target (ball) is large and comparatively slow moving.

Type 'A' personality	Type 'B' personality
Becomes stressed and uptight. Overworks in order to achieve.	*Tries to avoid the problem; e.g. does not do the task, or does it poorly.*
This child responds to stress by trying harder, tensing up, and generally becoming more uptight about the situation, trying harder and harder to work through it and achieve, despite the 'problem'.	This child subconsciously recognises the stress early on and rapidly develops avoidance strategies to minimise the impact upon themselves. The effort made to overcome the problem is minimal, and the stock response is avoidance.
The type A individual increases focus demands, suffers increasing near-point stress, and may show changes towards myopia, or short-sightedness. They may, however, simply suffer from migrainous type stress-related headaches, and show increasing loss of visual efficiency.	The type B individual may show difficulty in bringing material towards him-/herself, in effect minimising the near demands by denying the presence of objects close to him/her. This manifests (shows itself) as reduced focusing and poor convergence skills.

Learning Style.

Much has been written about learning style by others, but it is important that the child is allowed to use the style that suits them, whilst at the same time opportunities and encouragement are given to develop other learning styles. This may not be an easy task within a busy classroom, but should be a priority to implement. (Alistair Smith's book 'Accelerated learning in the classroom' ISBN1 85539 034 5 contains a great deal of information on learning styles.)

There are four main sensory channels of learning sight, sound, speech and movement. (Movement includes movements of hand/body/limbs, eyes, ears and the organs of speech.) Each of us also learns either mainly qualitatively or quantitatively, or a combination of the two. Qualitative learners see things as 'wholes' and like to move from one element of a task to another in a random way. Quantitative learners prefer to do things step-by-step.

Many children are lacking sufficient physical play in their early years, and this can later affect the development of higher skills that would otherwise have been triggered off by play.

Whilst a detailed programme of vision therapy should only ever be carried out under the guidance of an appropriately qualified professional, there are a number of simple activities that can be carried out safely at home, or in school, to help develop visual performance. However, Keith Holland has said "There is simply no substitute for a properly programmed and supervised course of vision therapy as the fastest and most thorough way to assist children with difficulties!" Much vision therapy is based on re-creating the sort of tasks that should have been carried out during early play that help foster visual co-ordination. These types of activities include eye movement and tracking tasks, left-right skills development and work on memory and sequencing.

Probably the commonest area of visual skill that can be helped at home, and that has a positive benefit for the child, is tracking (or eye movement work). In simple terms, the development of eye movements in children starts with the ability to maintain concentration on a target – such as the mother's face – for long enough that cognition (understanding) can occur. The ability to move the eyes around and follow a target, without having to involve the whole head and body in the movement, is a subsequent and important step. Whilst there are many other areas that can be effectively trained at home, these should only be attempted under professional guidance, and are therefore not included in this book.

Do not let this happen. A number of recent studies conducted in many countries have shown that visual difficulties are often fundamental causes of learning difficulties. If they can be spotted, and rectified, then many children can go on to fulfil their potential, and become successful members of society. If they are not dealt with, then the same studies have shown that they can lead to loss of self-esteem, behaviour difficulties, academic failure, and ultimately to delinquent behaviour. **Make this happen instead!**

PART 2

By Jan Poustie with acknowledgements to Keith Holland, the Institute of Optometry and Patricia Clayton, Irlen Centre South West. (See Appendix 1 for addresses of the relevant organisations which can supply further information regarding overlays and lenses and for information regarding orthoptists.)

COLOURED LENSES AND OVERLAYS

The choice of the route to effective provision in order to remediate the person's difficulties when visual and visual-perceptual difficulties are present is still regarded by some of the different specialists in the field as being controversial. Each of the routes relates to complementary aspects of functioning; e.g. Behavioural Optometry, the use of lenses/overlays via Irlen Filters or Cerium products and the strategies used by Orthoptists.

Much has been written recently about the beneficial effects of coloured lenses and contact lenses on individuals when Dyslexia is present. There is indeed research to support this and

At present an orthoptist assessment is available under the National Health Service (via one's GP) but colorimeter, behavioural optometry and Irlen Filters assessments are not. The price of these assessments varies with the colorimeter assessment being the cheapest. Despite the controversy that exists with regards to the different forms of treatment there appears to be no doubt that each can be effective for some students. It, therefore, seems very wrong that our children are not able to gain free access via the National Health Service to the 'aids/remediation programme' that they require in order to cope with literacy tasks.

readers interested in this area can contact the College of Optometrists (Tel: 0171 8396000) and the Institute of Optometry (Tel: 0171 4074183) for information on their use with regards to Meares-Irlen Syndrome. (Note: this condition is also known as Irlen Syndrome, Scotopic Sensitivity Syndrome and Scotopic Sensitivity Irlen Syndrome.) The Cerium precision-tinted lenses and Cerium overlays which are the aids used in the Intuitive Colorimeter assessment are regarded as appropriate by some specialists and the Irlen filters are regarded as appropriate by others.

Research conducted by Keith Holland has shown that individuals helped by colour usually have an underlying physical visual problem that is affecting learning, and that this needs to be tackled by an appropriate specialist. The advice from the Irlen Filters and the Intuitive Colorimeter specialists is that people who report perceptual distortion, or eye-strain, should first be examined by an optometrist to check the health of the eyes and to look for the visual difficulties described elsewhere in this chapter. Then any underlying physical visual problem should be assessed and treated first. However, if symptoms persist once such treatment has occurred then it may be wise to investigate the Irlen Filters or the Intuitive Colorimeter.

The Intuitive Colorimeter:
Information supplied by the Institute of Optometry (Tel: 020 7407 4183) and edited by Jan Poustie.
Research has shown that the distortion can sometimes be reduced, or eliminated, by wearing tinted spectacles. The appropriate colour varies from person to person, and to be effective the colour has to be chosen individually and with precision. Sometimes the colour gives an improvement in reading fluency; sometimes it simply helps a person to read for longer without eye-strain. The Intuitive Colorimeter can be used to prescribe coloured glasses for some people who experience certain problems whilst reading including Dyslexia, headache or visual discomfort. Treatment of visual problems should not be expected to cure Dyslexia but the treatment may, in some cases, make reading more comfortable.

One needs to judge the possible benefits of colour by using overlays first. These are coloured plastic sheets placed upon a page of text. A large number of differently coloured overlays should be compared, otherwise the most effective colour may be missed. If a particular colour reduces distortion and discomfort then an overlay can be given for a trial period to assess its effects. If the overlay is used consistently and is clearly beneficial, coloured glasses should be considered. Glasses are simpler to use, and the larger range of colour available with lenses may be helpful in obtaining the best effects. The most effective colour for use in overlays is not the same as that for use in spectacles.

Irlen Filters:
Information supplied by Patricia Clayton (Tel 01460 65555) and edited by Jan Poustie.
Scotopic Sensitivity Irlen Syndrome (also known as Meares-Irlen Syndrome) is a perceptual dysfunction affecting reading- and writing-based activities as well as depth perception. When this syndrome is present individuals put more energy and effort into the reading process

because they are inefficient readers who see the page differently from the 'good' reader. Constant adaptation to distortions from print or from the white background causes fatigue and discomfort and, more importantly, limits the length of time these individuals can read and maintain comprehension. When this syndrome goes undetected in individuals they may be viewed as underachievers with poor behavioural attitudes or motivational problems. They often appear bright but fail to produce a level of work that is considered appropriate for their age/intellect and may have been labelled 'stupid'.

The syndrome is caused by sensitivity to light rather than a visual problem of a refractive nature. Neurological research suggests that by selectively filtering the input of specific wavelengths of light, the Irlen Filter technique allows receptor cells in the visual cortex to analyse visual information more efficiently. Irlen Filters are specially modified filters that are beneficial to those who are inefficient readers, and may reduce symptoms of those suffering from eye-strain, headaches and migraine.

BRAIN RESEARCH
Over the last few years a great deal of research has been conducted into the brain. There have been several findings which indicate that there is a difference in the performance of the visual pathways of the brain. (Readers can see further information on this in the New Scientist dated 24th April 1999 – see Appendix 1 for details.) The more findings there are which support a visual difficulty as a major factor in Dyslexia the more likely we are to have yet further discussion as to the best ways of managing and overcoming such difficulties.

WHO IS LIKELY TO BE AFFECTED BY THESE DIFFICULTIES
It is important to note that visual and perceptual difficulties affect both children and adults. Parents and teachers also need to be aware that ME (also known as chronic/post-viral fatigue syndrome) can also cause a difference in functioning within the visual system. This can result in difficulties in reading stamina where the student may only be able to read for a few minutes at a time.

STRATEGIES THAT CAN HELP
Some children find coloured paper less glaring than white, and this may be established by trial and error, and used where appropriate. (The Institute of Optometry recommend that if an overlay is found to be useful for reading, then the presentation of written work may sometimes be improved by the use of coloured paper having a shade similar to the overlay.) The Barrington-Stokes range of reading books for children avoid 'glare' by deliberately using a creamy-buff coloured paper for the pages of their books (parents can access these via bookshops such as Waterstones). Sometimes, using a different colour of ink when writing/ printing out text from a computer can also be helpful for such students.

For many years, behavioural optometrists worldwide have used programmes of vision therapy to help children and adults improve visual function, and hence help overall achievement. In the past some of the exercise programmes have been difficult for parents to manage especially when Specific Learning Difficulty Profile conditions are present which affect behaviour; e.g. Dyspraxia, Attention Deficits and Autistic Spectrum Disorder. However, there are now tools available to behavioural optometrists which can make the exercise part of a programme easier for the parent to manage at home under a specialist's supervision; e.g. the HTS Home Vision Therapy System computer program.

Teaching Methods 1 and 4 mentioned in Appendix 2 are particularly effective when Occulomotor Delay/Dyspraxia is present.

Chapter 8

PLANNING AND ORGANISATIONAL DIFFICULTIES

(More strategies for these difficulties can be found in 'Planning and Organisation Solutions' by Jan Poustie, ISBN 1 901544 81 8.)

Any of the difficulties that accompany the conditions found in the Specific Learning Difficulties Profile will cause problems for the student when writing creatively, or factually. The problem is made worse when planning and organisational difficulties are present too. These difficulties seem to be part of all the conditions found within the Specific Learning Difficulties Profile. Students either have to have their world totally organised (and it must not change) as can be seen in Autistic Spectrum Disorder (and some individuals where Dyspraxia is present). Alternatively, they cannot organise their world at all (or it takes a huge effort to do so). Their lives, bedroom, house, workspace are always untidy until they have a 'blitz' but everything soon returns to its former state. This failure to organise (or only being able to cope with a certain way of organising) also affects one's ability to acquire literacy skills.

Poor planning & organisational skills cause frustration on the part of the student and those around him!

Classification

In order to access words from memory and to spell and read well we have to classify words. If 'word-finding' difficulties are present the student has a problem in finding the word in memory out of the thousands that are stored there. It is much easier if the word is associated with other words in our mind. Thus if we want 'shoe' we have to be able to classify it with other words and this gives us 'memory hooks' with which to extract the word from memory. However, this requires us to classify words into a variety of groups; e.g.

- types of shoe worn by different creatures: horseshoe, shoe
- an element of clothing for the foot: shoe, sock
- words used for 'shoe': plimsoll, trainer, shoe

Without classification skills each word is in its own pigeon-hole and unless we stumble across the right one in our search then it cannot be accessed.

The same need to classify applies to spelling and reading. We have to classify words into certain groups; e.g. those with a 'sp' sound at the beginning will always be spelt using the letters 'sp'. This saves us a lot of energy as we do not have to work out this pattern each time that we are faced with a 'sp' word. If we cannot classify we have to learn each word in isolation which makes tremendous demands on our memories. Every variation of a word also has to be learnt; e.g. spell, spells and spelling. Therefore, unless specialist SpLD provision is received, only extremely bright students who possess good visual imagery skills are likely to learn to spell and read if they lack, or have poor, classification skills.

Decision making

Some of these students have huge problems with decision making which makes all of their life very complicated and can drive parents and teachers to distraction. They cannot decide when to read the book in the evening. They cannot decide the plot of the story, which word to use in it, let alone which spelling of a particular sound blend is correct; e.g. both 'tian' (alsatian) and 'tion' (station) sound the same. (In this case it is fairly easy to solve the problem to a certain extent by telling them that 'tion' is used in the English language far more than 'tian'. So, when deciding which spelling to use they should write 'tion' as they have a greater chance of being right.)

Even deciding what to eat can be a difficult decision for some students!

 **Some people can get really 'bogged down' when it comes to making decisions.**

Decision making difficulties are made much worse when any of the forms of Attention Deficits are present. Such students can find it very difficult to settle to any task which requires mental effort unless they are really interested in the subject/task. Unfortunately, spelling, reading and writing may not be that interesting to them! This group can also 'plan' for ever in their mind and never actually settle down to the task. If they manage to start the task they may well never finish it.

THE EFFECTS ON SPELLING AND WRITING CAUSED BY A COMBINATION OF PLANNING AND ORGANISATIONAL/LANGUAGE AND MOVEMENT DIFFICULTIES

Some students have difficulties with spelling because they:

a   Cannot classify.

b   Cannot organise their thoughts and remember the spelling and/or the construction of the letters simultaneously. They literally go into 'overload' and cannot think straight.

c   Cannot decide which way of spelling the sound is right.

There are various ways of overcoming these difficulties. The book '*Planning and Organisation Solutions' (ISBN 1 901544 81 8)* provides plenty of advice on this and photocopiable masters that can be used in a home or educational setting. The main areas which need to be dealt with are:

1. IMPROVE GENERAL PLANNING, ORGANISATION AND CLASSIFICATION SKILLS

This can be achieved via the number version of the game 'Rummikub'. This is available from toy shops or from Next Generation. It needs to be played about four times a week for about six weeks.

2. ENABLE THE STUDENT TO THINK MORE CLEARLY

This can be achieved by using a planning and organisation strategy that suits his/her natural learning style.

3. IMPROVE THE STUDENT'S ORGANISATION OF THOUGHT

There are various strategies for this and it is a case of seeing which is effective for a particular student; e.g. many students find making a 'Mind Map' is very helpful here. 'Get ahead' by Vanda North and Tony Buzan (ISBN1 874374 00 7) is a very easy introduction to Mind Mapping. However, students and teachers really need to explore several methods of structuring stories to find out which suits the student best. Students with moderate to severe difficulties in knowing what is relevant when speaking/writing may benefit from a programme that the author heard of just before going to print – 'Language choices'. It is by Wendy Rinaldi and apparently, it is a programme that takes between one and two years to complete (available Tel: 01483 458411).

4. REDUCE THE STUDENT'S EFFORT

If the amount of effort required by the student is reduced, a higher quality/longer story can be achieved.

- Let the student dictate the story onto a tape recorder. (This can be an especially effective method for students when Attention Deficits is present.) An adult types up the story and then the student edits it. Computer dictation programs are not suitable for this strategy as the student cannot dictate the story fast enough and keep the plot/sentence construction in memory whilst dictating. (Note: When Specific Language Impairment is present students may experience oral expressive language/ pronunciation difficulties which may make this strategy unsuitable for them.)

- The student draws the story using a series of cartoons with speech bubbles for small amounts of text. This especially suits the visual learner and students who, like Attention Deficits students, require a quick result. A similar result using a single page cartoon and speech bubbles can be created using the 'Storymaker' (see page A32). This program would especially suit students with drawing difficulties (e.g. when Graphomotor Dyspraxia is present).

Using small amounts of text written in speech bubbles attached to stick animals and people can reduce the writing task and make it more interesting to the student.

•The younger student could write the story using a word processor such as 'Kid Works Deluxe' for PC/Mac (available from Havas Interactive UK Ltd Tel: 01752 206010) or some of the 'Widgit' software (see page A32) where they can click on an icon (little picture) and the word appears on the screen. Another type of word processor which is useful is 'Storybook Weaver' where the child creates a picture first. In the older 'classic' version of this programme the student then clicks on various parts of the screen and as s/he does so words are transferred to the typing part of the screen. 'Clicker' is also useful as it enables the student to click on a word/phrase on the screen which is then inserted into his sentence. 'Talking Pendown' (Acorn – See page A32) is a more conventional type of word processor which can be used by a wide age group. Older students could use 'Widgit' or 'Clicker' or an adult word processor/desktop publishing program. Microsoft Publisher is particularly easy to use – it is the program that has been used to publish this book.

ouse	ound	oud
mouse	hound	cloud
house	round	
	pound	Fig. 1

5.   IMPROVE CLASSIFICATION SKILLS

This can be done by teaching variations of a pattern; e.g. 'ouse, ound, oud'. First the tutor writes the following words onto separate cards: mouse, house, found, hound, round, cloud, pound. A strip of card is placed on the table with the sounds on it. The student has to say the word and then place the card in a column below the correct sound as shown in Fig. 1.

Once students are used to the task the tutor can:

A   Increase the number of cards by introducing new words that fit the pattern

B   Time how long it takes them to complete the task and see if they can do it faster next time. (Always give them a 'long minute' so that they do not lose. Do not time them if they are at all anxious about the task, or, are naturally anxious children. Those with Attention Deficits may like the idea of a timed task as long as they win but can become very angry if they lose!)

C   Ask the student to do the task and then write down all the words in one of the columns. If this is made a race by the student against the tutor this activity can be a big boost to the student's self-esteem. This can be achieved if:
- the student is allowed to start writing before the tutor
- the tutor has to think of several other words to add to each list
- the tutor only just manages to lose the race.

6.   REDUCE THE DECISION-MAKING ASPECT OF WRITING THE STORY.

The following technique also avoids the problem of difficulties in starting the writing task by giving the student a choice between two different happenings at each point in the story. This sort of technique would also help those students who may lack, or have weak, imagination skills as is likely to occur when Autistic Spectrum Disorder is present and can occur when

Attention Deficits is present. This technique would enable the student to write an interesting story. It is likely to be more interesting if pictures are also provided as shown here.

A	This story is about a red dragon
	or
B	This story is about a red car
A	The dragon/car was lonely so he
	or
B	The dragon/car was sad so he
A tried to find some friends.	
or	
B went on an adventure.	

This story is about a big red dragon called Harry. He was so very lonely that he cried all day. He joined the cubs and found lots of friends.

7. REDUCE THE DEMANDS ON DECISION-MAKING AND IMAGINATIVE SKILLS

Some students have difficulties in decision making and/or in using their imagination. (The former can occur when Attention Deficits is present and the latter can occur with both Attention Deficits and Autistic Spectrum Disorder.)

As shown on the right, the student has the plot virtually worked out for him. He has to choose either statement A or B each time and then supply the descriptive words. Different strategies can help the student decide what to write; e.g. tossing a coin just before he writes each statement (heads – he chooses A etc.) or the tutor could say you are choosing all A's/B's/alternate A's & B's etc. Different stories could be written using different A and B sentences and the student could also be encouraged to include names for the characters and descriptive words; e.g. This story is about a big, red and <u>very handsome</u> dragon <u>called Harry</u>.

Case Study – Adam, a 9-year-old student (Attention Deficits was present.)
Adam was finding it very difficult to write about the feelings of the church congregation when Princess (later Queen) Victoria was christened. Her drunk uncle changed her name at the christening without the agreement of her parents. (When Attention Deficits, or Autistic Spectrum Disorder, are present students can find it very difficult to put themselves 'into the shoes' of other people.) Setting the scene verbally via a picture, or via a Mind Map, is a very useful strategy for such students; and for those for whom written expressive language difficulties are causing problems.) The tutor used several strategies to personalise the event and then enable him to relate to it. She:

1. Talked about an incident which had just happened to her. She had taken a group of children to Weston-Super-Mare when suddenly a citizen's arrest was made in front of them. The criminal pushing past the group in his attempt to escape startled everyone, confused them and worried the younger members of the group.
2. She then asked Adam how he would have reacted in this situation and how he felt his mother might have reacted and what they might have said.
3. The tutor verbally 'set the scene' in the church asking questions at each point. Everybody dressed in their best clothes and then the drunk uncle arriving – "Would people be concerned if someone who was drunk entered his school's chapel?" The parent's had already chosen a different name – "Would they be startled/surprised when a new name was given?" etc.

 Creating the picture first can give students a 'visual hook' on which to focus their thoughts and construct their sentences. When fine motor difficulties are present students should be provided with the picture (e.g. computer clip art). Those who are very artistic should be encouraged to produce a 'quick' drawing as the picture is the means by which the text is produced and helps us to understand the story. Thus, unlike in an art lesson, the picture is not the part which is being marked.

Chapter 9

Behaviour and literacy
(including Autistic Spectrum Disorder and Asperger Syndrome)

There are many aspects to behaviour, and several of the Specific Learning Difficulties Profile conditions have large behavioural elements; e.g. Autistic Spectrum Disorder (ASD) and Attention Deficits (ADD). Behavioural differences also accompany Dyspraxia which is often associated with the presence of hyperactivity with Attention Deficits (ADHD). A level of social immaturity compared with the individual's peer group is commonly seen alongside Dyspraxia. The effects on literacy of Attention Deficits and Dyspraxia have already been dealt with in chapters 3 and 4. When Dyspraxia and Attention Deficits are present we may also see elements of ASD e.g. Autistic Tendencies. This chapter has been included to give the reader some idea of the behavioural problems that occur when ADD or an element of ASD are present, and to offer some strategies that can be tried. The strategies in this section are not meant to replace specialist advice but they may be found useful whilst the adults involved with the student are in the process of finding out information from specialist agencies mentioned in Appendix 1. Professionals can also find out information via their Local Education Authority (LEA) special advisors on students with behavioural/ communication difficulties. In more enlightened authorities parents have access to these advisors too (they can be accessed via the Education Department at the county's headquarters which is often called 'County Hall'). Unless the environmental conditions meet the student's needs, learning will not take place at the appropriate rate. Those 'needs' include a variety of factors as shown below:

 It is important to remember that each student is unique and has a unique set of difficulties, weaknesses and strengths. We have to use the strengths to overcome the student's difficulties.

UNUSUAL SENSITIVITIES TO SENSORY INFORMATION
These are associated with the presence of Dyspraxia and Autistic Spectrum Disorder. Students can be hypersensitive to texture, smell, taste, noise etc. They may become distressed when touching the wax crayons, plastic desk or the sandpaper letters which are sometimes used for teaching the alphabet. They may find unpleasant the smell of the teacher's aftershave/perfume or the cleansers used in the classroom. The sound of the fire alarm can be particularly frightening and they may become confused/refuse to leave the building along a route not normally used; e.g. through the fire door. Alternatively, they may become fascinated by the gentle movements of the streamer hanging from the ceiling and watch it for hours; lights, a moving part of machinery, the sound of a pen scratching on paper can be equally riveting.

MANAGING THE STUDENT IN THE CLASSROOM
It is important to remember that what will work with one student will not work with another. Adults faced with dealing with such students may realise that they need to prevent the difficulties occurring but feel that specialist knowledge is needed in order to do so. Specialist advice may not be that easy to obtain.

Case Study – Seven-year-old boy (Asperger Syndrome, Dyspraxia and Attention Deficits)
The author recently learnt of a case where a child was very distressed at the end of his first day at his local junior school. His teacher had been shouting at him a lot because he was not listening – never an easy task for a student when this group of difficulties is present. He was

kept in at break because he had not finished his work. The headteacher told the parent that a meeting between the Special Educational Needs Co-ordinator (SENCO, also sometimes known as AENCO), the class teacher and the parent could not be arranged for a fortnight. The mother was worried sick, as her son had become aggressive in a previous school when he was unable to cope with the teacher's handling of him. On his second day at school she had a great struggle to get him into school and feared that by the end of the next week she would not be able to get him into school at all.

When ASD and ADD are present students can have great difficulties in staying motivated long enough to finish (and sometimes to even start) tasks. Attention Deficit students find it particularly difficult to stay on task when mental effort is required. Dyspraxia can cause the student to write very slowly and this too can make task completion difficult. This student's set of difficulties meant that finishing his work would have been an unusual achievement rather than the normal one for him! Keeping him in to finish his work was not a solution; instead the task itself needed to be changed so enabling him to complete it. Thus towards the end of the task he could have been asked to complete it orally, or the whole/part of the task could have required completion in a more practical manner, using pictures etc. ADD and ASD students are likely to find it difficult to cope with the teacher shouting at them or shouting at other children in the class. They may find it so distressing that they refuse to go to school or feel ill before going to school in the morning.

The ADD student can find it difficult to stay on task (especially when mental effort is required).

This parent tried to access her local authority's Special Educational Needs Support Team but was instead transferred to her Local Education Authority's (LEA) Parent Partnership Officer. This official can be helpful in some cases but where a school is not being co-operative in the management of/provision for a student they lack any powers to make them be so. The LEA advisor for children with communication difficulties was accessed. He informed the parent that he could not become involved because her son did not have a Statement of Special Educational Needs. This raises a serious issue. If LEA's do not want the vast expense of parent's attempting to obtain a Statement for their child as the only way of gaining appropriate support for them then children without statements will need to be appropriately provided for. It can cost an authority £2000+ to process a student (for the assessments, meetings etc.) when a Statement is applied for, plus a great deal of time on the part of a variety of professionals. During this stage there is often a great deal of stress for the family and student (both of whom may lack appropriate provision at this time).

TOPIC/TASK CHOICE AND STRATEGIES

ASD students in particular have difficulties in producing written work/taking on information etc. which is not related to their own areas of interest. (ADD students may also have such difficulties.) Making the work relevant to the student can be helpful when trying to overcome this problem; e.g. if the student likes Star Wars then relate topics to it. So if the class is doing a topic on suitable environments for frogs let the student write on 'Whether the planet Hoth was a suitable environment for frogs and how could Luke Skywalker improve it for them'. Similarly, if the student has an obsession with the Second World War relate his/her work to that topic when first introducing it and try to steer the work from the subject of the obsession to a wider field (so that we extend the student's areas of interest) as in the following example. If the topic is 'theatres of war in the Second World War' we can look at:

☐ North Africa and tank warfare
☐ South Africa and the Boer War
☐ Geographical features that affected both wars etc.

If students refuse to read the books in the school reading scheme, alternative reading materials can be found by using their area of interest. One girl (who had Asperger Syndrome) started school, read a few books from the class reading scheme, and then flatly refused to read any more. It was suggested that her interest in maths was used to enable her to make progress in her reading. After all, there are plenty of very easy maths books around; e.g. the Usborne early number workbooks (available from High Street bookshops) could be tried in this case.

Calendar and numerical information is often of great interest; e.g. dimensions of UK cathedrals, the dates of every Manchester United football match. When this is the case, we can enable the student to achieve success by directing his/her work towards this aspect of learning. The importance of relating information that has to be known/learnt to the student cannot be understated. Homework instructions may be disregarded when they are being given out unless the student is enabled to relate to the information. Homework may also not be done.

It is important for adults to be aware that there may be little awareness of social hierarchy. When this occurs the teacher (and any other adult) is no more important than any other human being (including even young children). Therefore, there is no reason to obey him/her.

POINTS TO NOTE

1. Abstract thinking may be well developed in the ASD student but making inferences may not – this is linked to the inability to imagine a situation and the Theory of Mind. (Other language-impaired students may also have a similar difficulty.) LDA produce sets of 'Reading for Comprehension' cards which can help here. Difficulties in achieving tasks which require imagination can occur, especially when ASD is present, and some ADD students also find this difficult too. Some students may have limited skills in certain areas but may not be able to transfer those skills to other areas of their lives. Some may be able to put themselves into 'other people's shoes' using the strategy mentioned on page 62 and they may be able to develop an acknowledgement, or some understanding, of the feelings of other people. (This awareness may occur in ADD students once the 'executive function' in the frontal lobe of the brain matures; e.g. towards the end of puberty or once their functioning is supported via medication. Puberty usually occurs later for boys than for girls. This later maturing can put the ADD boy at a severe disadvantage during the key years of his schooling.)

2. When ASD or ADD are present the student may be quite egocentric and so appear self-centred. S/he is likely to have lots of 'needs' rather than 'wants'.

3. Verbal skills may be highly advanced in the ASD student– so s/he may have a very good vocabulary. However, auditory comprehension in such students may be very weak and allowance will need to be made for this in conversation/teaching etc. Other students may have a written comprehension level which is more compatible with their verbal skills.

4. The student is likely to find it difficult to cope with disorganised sensory information; e.g. people moving around in a random way, items not displayed in a uniform way (according to their concept of what uniformity and randomness mean etc.). Bizarre behaviours can result from this; e.g. being unable to cope with the change of texture where a carpet-edging strip joins two pieces of carpet. The combination of Autism and Tuberous Sclerosis caused one particularly obsessive teenage girl to spend several hours one night rocking the toilet off the floor!!!! This behaviour occurred because one of the screws was loose. So, it really does pay to keep the general maintenance of the student's environment up to scratch!

5. Ritualistic behaviours are common in the ASD population and need to be fulfilled by the student in order for him/her to feel secure. Trying to change (or stop) the ritual merely results

in another ritual taking its place. Rituals can be very frustrating for the student's carer as the student can sometimes take a very long time to complete the whole ritual before any meaningful work can be started. (Interrupting the ritual is only likely to make the student start from the beginning again!)

6. ASD is characterised by difficulties in establishing normal effective relationships with people (including teachers and peer group). One consequence of this is that group work may be impossible for the student as s/he may just be an 'onlooker' or may wander off and do his/her 'own thing'. ASD children may be thinking of concepts/areas of information that are far beyond the interests of their peer group, and their originality of thought enables them to form their own theories. These students' originality, level of thinking and their different approach to life etc. may make them appear eccentric and this in turn increases their difficulties in relating to their peers and vice versa.

7. Teachers can feel overwhelmed when dealing with an ASD (or an ADD) student. The teacher's need to control and the student's inability to meet the teacher's needs can result in frequent conflict between teacher and student (and the student's parents) which further worsens the situation. The answering back (or the muttering under his/her breath) which can occur when the student does not want to do a task, can increase this level of conflict.

8. Routines and the need for 'sameness' (e.g. an unchanging environment and unchanging tasks) are exceptionally important to some students. Although some ADD individuals (such as the author) detest anything which appears to be of a routine nature, most ASD and ADD students do not cope well without routine. ASD students, in particular, require their world to be unchanging. Such students are likely to find it very difficult to cope when a supply teacher has to cover for their own teacher. Special events that change routine; e.g. sports day, may cause stress and unwanted behaviours. Therefore, both ADD and ASD students tend to function better when events happen at expected times and the requirements of the tasks do not change. When ASD is present it is especially necessary to inform students even of changes in lesson structure before they occur. Both groups of students need to be warned well in advance of changes and pictorial reminders on an easy-to-understand calendar can be useful here. (It should be noted that ASD students may have difficulties in understanding terms such as yesterday, today, tomorrow, before, after etc. Therefore, the reminder of the change will also have to occur the morning of the event and just before the event as well.)

The need for 'sameness' affects the ASD student's handling of changes in the environment. Thus, even different types of methods of gaining entrance to a building that s/he has not experienced before can be a problem for these students. Unfamiliar buildings may require the student to use automatic doors, escalators, lifts and different types of door handle (e.g. lever or knob).

9. It is often not realised that stress is a major cause of behavioural difficulties and this is especially the case when the student's needs have not been provided for adequately. Stress also causes the student to function less well academically and to also require 'sameness' in the environment and tasks. Thus, any student whose needs are not being met is likely to function better when in a structured environment and when s/he knows what to expect in a lesson/task.

10. ASD students are likely to produce their best work when they produce it in their own way. They are likely to perform badly when the task has to be done in a set way or they have to produce work using knowledge that has been learnt; e.g. in tests/examinations. Unfortunately for us, these students appear to only be able to experience the world (and the information that we present to them) in their own original way. Group work based tasks with their need for co-operation, acknowledgement of other people's needs/ideas and the ability to

work together as part of a team may be impossible for these students to achieve. ASD students are likely to find learning from others (including the teacher) difficult. Teachers who believe that their function is to impart knowledge (rather than to enable students to learn knowledge in their own way) are immediately in a conflict situation.

11. The ASD (and the ADD) student may distract others unless in a very organised and

 When Dyspraxia, ASD or ADD are present hand-written work may be poorly presented. If this is the case the student should be enabled to produce the bulk of his/her work via a computer program.

structured environment. Staying at his/her desk may also be very difficult for him/her.

12. The perception of the student by the parents and the teacher may be very different. Thus, when Asperger Syndrome, ADD or ASD are present, the parent may see a particularly bright child whilst the teacher may only see a child who is not living up to his expectations. The teacher expects the child to sit still, pay attention, answer questions, learn the subject he is teaching and score well in examinations. However, a student affected by these conditions may be unable to meet these expectations, or will find it very difficult to do so. In an educational setting the Asperger Syndrome student (and the anxious student) may need to interact with those around them in order to feel secure and to acquire knowledge; e.g. via constant questioning of peer group and adults. However, the teacher wants his/her students to acquire knowledge in a more passive way; e.g. through reading etc. A way of overcoming this problem, and enabling the students to learn, might be to put all those students who need to question together in a small group at the end of the classroom so that discussions can take place without distracting the rest of the class. This group of students would need to include the 'global/qualitative learners' mentioned in Chapter 7 who also need to use questions as a means of learning.

13. ASD affects both the learning process and what the student is prepared to learn. The student may easily grasp abstract concepts. As long as intellectual functioning is normal, or above average,

ADD and ASD students do not like to be distracted from their own thoughts. So directing their attention to the topic under class discussion etc. may not be easy.

there may be a good intellectual grasp of the world, but whereas the rest of the class will follow the lead of the teacher the ASD student has to follow his/her own path. The blinkered attitude and interests which results from this can in some cases lead to exceptional achievement in the chosen area of study. This can occur because, unlike the rest of us, such students may not be distracted from studying because of a need to socialise with peers etc.

14. Adults need to be aware that what we expect to happen with ASD students may not necessarily occur. Thus, for most students, copying spellings from a blackboard (which uses short-term memory) is easier than writing the words from dictation (which is a long-term memory retrieval task). However, Hans Asperger noted that the opposite can be true of Asperger Syndrome students. Generally speaking, however, many ASD students will have difficulties with phonological skills, and both copying and writing from dictation will result in many misspelled words. Visual-perceptual difficulties can be seen alongside ASD and Dyspraxia (see Chapter 4 for further information on such problems).

15. ASD students need to create everything out of their own thoughts and experience and so mechanical methods of learning are unlikely to work for them. ADD students may have similar needs. Thus the Phonological Awareness Training packs which are an effective means for improving the spelling ability of many children are not likely to be an effective learning tool for such students. However, phonological strategies such as the 'sounding out'

of the parts of a word can be learnt by some ASD students. The various planning and organisational tools that can be found in 'Planning and organisation Solutions', see page A33, could be explored here. (This book provides details of many ways by which the student can organise information including spellings. The student will also need to be enabled to connect the various spelling patterns to information that relates to him/herself.)

16. Literacy tasks must be chosen with care when an element of ASD is present as the writing of jokes, humorous and/or imaginative stories may be difficult/impossible for the student. If reading does not interest the student then there can be major problems in acquiring and using this skill. Teachers need to be aware that there may be a wide range of performance in reading. Thus, whilst the reading accuracy of some students may be weak their reading comprehension may be good to excellent. (This can also occur when other SpLD Profile conditions are present.) Often teachers place students at a particular point on a reading scheme on the basis of their reading accuracy in a reading test. This would be inappropriate for this group of students. If the teacher does not place the student according to his/her comprehension ability then the result is likely to be a student who resists reading the reading scheme books because the text is not advanced enough.

SUCCESSFUL STUDENT MANAGEMENT
This is more likely to be achieved if the teacher remains calm – no easy task at times! The adult also needs to be in control of the student in an environment where there is the least amount of sensory stimulation. Just telling the student 'to concentrate' is not going to be effective. Unfortunately, telling the student off for not concentrating is also unlikely to be effective as it is likely to just result in a stressed child, teacher and parent. Strategies need to be found to help the student to concentrate. An independent study carrel (where the student's desk is shielded from distractions on three sides) can be useful when a task requiring written work is required. Long-term rewards (e.g. praise at the end of the lesson) are not likely to work, especially for young children. However, short-term rewards of praise for staying on task by placing a counter in a beaker (well attached to the desk) every time the teacher walks by may be more successful.

> If reading interests the student then s/he may learn to read at a very young age.

Care will be needed in the placement of the carrel; e.g. place it away from moving children, the teacher talking, doorways and windows. However, some ASD students panic if they are too far away from a doorway as they feel trapped. Such children could be either placed by the firedoor (and shown how it operates) or be placed to one side of the door where there will be the least amount of traffic. A placement with perhaps one desk between them and the door so that they do not see the movement of people travelling through the door out of corner of their eye as they work may be suitable. It should be noted that ASD (and ADD) students may be distracted by sounds etc. that the rest of us do not notice; e.g. the sounds of the water passing through a radiator.

Adults can find it very difficult to resolve the conflict when a student says that s/he no longer wants to do the task. Hans Asperger (in his original paper translated in 'Autism and Asperger syndrome' edited by Uta Frith) suggested that a variety of strategies can work including:
- Verbally agree with the student and just continue with the task as though the conversation had never occurred.
- There appears to be less resistance to doing the work/following the instructions if the teacher uses the same voice tone and pitch that the student uses.
- Issue commands instead of making polite requests of the student. Thus "I would like you to ……….." may not result in the required action but "Now you will do ………." is more likely to be effective.

Case Study: Girl A (ASD present)
The mother of Girl A found the following strategy worked with her child. She said to the child: "Imagine that we as a family need to push a boulder across the road. The rest of the family are pushing the boulder from the back but you are pushing it from the side or the front." (A concrete demonstration at this point can help the student to see that the boulder is going to have problems in moving forward when people are pushing it from different directions.) The mum went on to tell her child that "We need you to help us push the boulder from the same direction that we are pushing it from."

This case study also shows how the rest of the class can help the student achieve success if they co-operate with the teacher and the child. Thus the class was told by the teacher that Girl A was going to try to work independently. All the members of the class tried really hard not to fidget and to be quiet so that they helped the child concentrate on the task. She managed to concentrate for fifteen minutes and received a round of applause from her classmates for doing so.

GULLIBILITY AND SEXUALITY
Both ASD and ADD students are vulnerable to having their behaviour being misinterpreted. Their gullibility may result in them becoming the stooge for a gang and not seeing where the gang's actions are leading them, and thus they may do whatever they are told to do by the members of the gang.

Those the behavioural conditions found within the SpLD Profile are present students may have various difficulties relating to sex. Some of these difficulties can be seen quite young and others will carry on into adulthood. Some individuals may have difficulties with understanding and accepting their own sexuality – their first sexual experience (with or without intercourse) may frighten them. Others may greet headlong their emergent sexuality at puberty and thus be at risk of getting themselves into a situation of intimacy beyond that with which they feel comfortable. Of course, impulsive Attention Deficit individuals may rush into the relationship, may find controlling their sexual urges difficult and may explore their sexuality early. Their impulsivity and forgetfulness may also result in a failure to use contraceptives.

ASD students may demonstrate inappropriate and unconventional ways of satisfying their sexual needs which may often not involve other people. Students can form a sexual attachment to a physical object – fortunately as their behaviour may not be recognisably sexual to the onlooker it may have little impact upon the other students. Any object within the student's environment can be the focus for such attachment and attention; e.g. the plastic cover of their reading book which can be stroked or rubbed against their skin. Such behaviours may continue to occur or they may die down of their own accord. If such behaviours continue to occur the peer group may be happily oblivious to the implications of what is happening near them. However, the adult in charge of the student may find such behaviours rather disturbing and so may wish to access specialist advice. Mark Segar (an adult who has Asperger Syndrome) has written a book called 'A guide to Coping, Specifically for People with Asperger Syndrome'. It contains do's and don'ts for sexual behaviour and relationships and can be obtained from: The Early Years Centre, Publications Department, 272 Longdale Lane, Ravenshead, Nottingham NG15 9AH.

STRATEGIES FOR HELPING THE STUDENT WHO HAS REACHED AN 'OVERLOAD' SITUATION
Students are in this situation when they become overwhelmed by the task/environment. Overload situations need to be handled in different ways according to the individual student and the SpLD Profile conditions present. ASD students are likely to need pictorial/written

69

reminders which show them how they need to behave in certain situations which can occur regularly; e.g. s/he wants the radio turned off when the sound of it becomes distressing. Students in an overload situation may exhibit one of several behaviours; e.g.

• Withdraw
• Become frozen
• Behave in such a way that the adult feels forced to take control of the situation.

In the ASD student this behaviour may take the form of 'screaming' and other unusual behaviours whilst both ASD and ADD students may interfere with another child's toys etc. Carers tend to respond to the student's behaviour rather than the trigger which caused the behaviour. Thus the carer may try (usually without much success) to control (or ignore) the behaviour and expect this to resolve the problem.

Students need to be taught ways to tell the carer/brothers/sisters etc. that they are overwhelmed. Initially this may be done by using a strategy such as coloured cards based on the colours of the traffic lights which has three stages.

Stage 1

Red indicates "I am very overwhelmed, can't cope – I'm at a stop". Yellow indicates "I'm feeling upset and going to stop soon". Green indicates that all is well.

Stage 2

We want to progress the student to communicating their problems in a more adult and socially acceptable way, which means via language, as soon as possible. So we write words on the cards and the adult states these words to the student when he shows a card e.g. red – 'very upset', yellow – 'starting to feel upset', green 'okay'. When the student is not upset the adult could explain that these are the words that she wants the student to use when s/he is upset; e.g. "I am very upset". The adult now encourages the student to show the card and/or read the words. *(Note: some ASD students cannot talk, or elect not to do so. When this occurs there will be a need for the student, and those working with him/her, to learn an alternative communication system. Contact the National Autistic Society for further information – see Appendix 1 for details.)*

Stage 3

Some students may progress to this stage. Here they are encouraged to explain the problem in greater detail. The student could have a series of red and yellow cards which have a picture/word on the front which explains the problem; e.g. noise (an ear), other children/ students (people), movement, too hot, too much of too many things etc. Eventually the student may be able to tell the carer the problem rather than showing the appropriate card.

Cards could be kept in school in a special container which is attached to the desk with blutak. At home, cards could be kept in a bag which is worn around the student's waist or they could be attached to a key ring on a belt etc. Attaching the cards together is likely to be sensible as it will stop the student becoming frustrated if the cards are dropped when showing them to the adult. If the student is not located in one classroom then a set of these cards should be in every classroom. Every teacher in the school should know the location of the cards as this will then help the teacher who has to 'cover' for the usual teacher when illness occurs etc.

★ ★ ★

The Picture Exchange Communication System (PECS) can be used in a similar way to the traffic lights cards to produce an individualised communication package for any age. It is suitable for a variety of situations; e.g. displaying the timetable for the day and providing the student with an individualised package (via an individual folder which the student takes from classroom to classroom etc.). It uses words and picture symbols which are attached via velcro to a board etc. This system is available from Pyramid Educational Consultants Inc, 226 West Park Place, Suite 1, Newark, DE 19711, USA Tel: 00 888 732 7462 (website: www.pecs.com). The use of this system can result in the student making tremendous strides in communication, increasing their vocabulary and the amount of speech used as well as leading to an improvement in behaviour.

HAVING A GREATER UNDERSTANDING OF THE STUDENT'S DIFFICULTIES
We tend to understand better if we can have some personal experience of the problem. Thus all those who deal with a student at home (and at school etc.) may benefit from a demonstration of what it is like to be overloaded by sensory information; e.g.
- the radio up really loud whilst someone is shouting an instruction to them
- the TV and the radio up really loud and the group trying to follow what is on the TV whilst someone is moving in front of it etc.

(Be very careful that you do not use flickering lights as a part of any such demonstration as this can cause problems for students affected by epilepsy. Care will also need to be taken to ensure that no student/adult is present who is hypersensitive to high levels of the sensory information being used in the demonstration. The demonstration should obviously occur when the ASD student is not in the room.)

CONDUCTING A 'RISK ASSESSMENT'
It is obviously better to avoid problems before they start. Therefore, the wise teacher/learning support assistant will want to know:
- what situations are likely to cause the student to have difficulties
- what the student's interests are etc. before s/he enters the classroom.

A 'risk assessment' with the parent/s prior to the student being introduced to any new situation may be worth its weight in gold.

In industry, staff conduct a 'risk assessment' when looking at health and safety issues. Similarly, in education the wise carer will conduct a 'risk assessment' to reduce behavioural difficulties/stress to the student before introducing him/her to the new situation. Only by being aware of how the student is likely to react can the carer devise strategies that may be successful in overcoming the problem. Professionals may have to accept that the 'expert' to whom they can turn for a great deal of useful information here (including strategies that might work) is likely to be the mum and dad!

REFERRALS AND SUPPORTIVE AGENCIES
When behavioural difficulties are present and advice on management is required then the student should be referred via his/her GP to the appropriate specialists; e.g. to one of the following local agencies/specialists:
- Child Development Centre
- Community paediatrician
- Communication Disorder Clinic
- A specialist centre such as the Newcomen Centre at Guy's Hospital, London.

Diagnosis for Dyspraxia, Attention Deficits and Autistic Spectrum Disorder are made via the medical sector. However, it is the teachers, special needs support assistants etc. who have to cope in the educational setting with the problems that such conditions can cause in learning and in the classroom. Effective management of these students requires good and frequent liaison between the educational and medical professionals and between educational establishments and specialist Local Education Authority advisors. Unfortunately this does not always occur.

The author learned recently of a headmaster who was admitting a new student into his school. Although the headteacher knew that Aspergers Syndrome was present he chose not to bring in any support/provide a knowledge base for the teacher regarding the condition. When the teacher requested such support she was told that she was a good teacher and 'would cope'. Such an attitude was likely to result in stress and frustration for the teacher, the student and the parent.

Support

Professionals need to be aware that the behaviours caused by the presence of Attention Deficits and Autistic Spectrum Disorder can make even the best of parents appear unable to cope. These parents, and those of the student who has Dyspraxia, can pass from one embarrassing moment to the next on a frequent basis (daily if they are lucky, hourly if they are not). Parent's suffer from temper tantrums in Marks and Spencers (with onlookers saying "Tut, tut – I never let my children behave like that"). They can have mother-in-laws telling them that they must be firmer, that they are spoiling the child. They face the embarrassment of the odd full glass of ice-cold coke cascading down the businessman's suit at the Little Chef, followed by the fork and the food landing on the floor. (All these behaviours are due to poor co-ordination skills and nervousness in a new situation.)

Parents may dread receiving the phone call from school for yet another meeting where they are taken to task for their child's behaviour. If the school does not understand the conditions then staff can feel threatened. The parent may have had to learn a great deal about the condition, and how to manage it, but fears upsetting the professionals. This fear can be present throughout every meeting parents have with the professionals. Parents may fear rejection when asking for their child to be treated differently from other children even though that differentiation is both their child's right and 'their need'. They watch their child became less and less happy at school and, because of the stress of the academic environment, the child becomes more and more difficult to handle at home. The final straw for many parents is when they are viewed by professionals as being incompetent, lacking in discipline, demanding or having unrealistic academic goals for their child. (Professionals can easily assume the latter when the SpLD Profile conditions mask average or superior intelligence.)

When any of the conditions mentioned in this chapter are present, students can be 'testing' for the most competent, knowledgeable and able professional. All those involved (whether parent, professional or other carer) need to support each other. When the student's behaviours are particularly difficult to manage there should be, whenever possible, 'time out breaks' where the adult is enabled to be away from the student for a period of time. Such breaks may be essential when the teacher has the student for the whole of the school day as can occur in primary schools.

Support can be obtained from a variety of sources; e.g. the local group of the relevant UK national charity can provide support for both parents and professionals (see Appendix 1 for details). Various agencies offer family guidance which can help the whole family to cope with the presence of behavioural difficulties; e.g. social services and the NSPCC (their telephone numbers will be in the family's local telephone directory). Family Guidance can provide parents with someone to talk to on a regular basis and can provide feedback and support. The presence of any of the SpLD Profile conditions can have an impact upon other family members and here 'Contact-a-family' is a useful organisation as it provides support meetings for the brothers and sisters of the student. (Their telephone number will be in the family's local telephone directory.)

Conclusion

It is easy for all those concerned to greet the diagnosis of Dyslexia with despair and to feel that success in literacy-based tasks cannot be achieved. This is not the case as long as we provide effective and appropriate support as early as possible. Even if the student only receives adequate support late in life s/he may still be enabled to obtain his/her life goals.

CHANGING OUR PERSPECTIVE OF DYSLEXIA

There is also an alternative way of viewing Dyslexia which can change our perception of it. All the conditions found within the Specific Learning Difficulties Profile seem to have various common elements; i.e. difficulties in the perception of certain areas of information, the classification of that information, its organisation and its prioritisation. One explanation of the appearance of these difficulties in the human species may be reflected in the frequent appearance of increased creativity found in so many of the individuals who have these conditions. If a person lacks organisation of information in any area then s/he will have difficulties in understanding and using it unless s/he can impose his/her own form of order upon it. Consequently, those who have the greatest difficulty in creating order will have the greatest difficulty in gaining academic and life skills. Imposing one's own order upon information requires original and innovative thinking. Without original thought, and the innovations associated with it, the human species could not evolve. Books have been written about the Gifts of Dyslexia but it may be that our perception is at fault here. Perhaps those who have the conditions found within the Specific Learning Difficulties Profile do not have a Gift of Dyslexia but are themselves Nature's Gift to the human species without whom we could not evolve so fast!

Two of the most moving moments in one parent's life was seeing (lying on the bed of her dyslexic daughter) a book with which she had read herself to sleep and the huge smile on her daughter's face when she was able to sing a song by reading the words just like everyone else rather than by having to remember them. Professionals working with students who have a wide range of specific learning difficulties know that their work is worthwhile when the 'lines of strain' on both the parent and the student begin to reduce and the student actually starts to smile in the lesson too! For far too many students literacy tasks are unrewarding. Reading a book is never relaxing. Trying to write their thoughts (whilst spelling the words correctly enough and writing legibly enough so that someone else can read it) is one more chore in life and little pleasure is found in the learning environment. If one has a broken leg then one cannot walk. Not being able to walk will not be resolved until the underlying problem (the fracture) is dealt with. Similarly, it seems that Dyslexia needs to be viewed as the reflection of the differences in structure and function of the brain and, therefore, we have to deal with these underlying differences if we are to succeed in improving the student's literacy functioning. It appears then that the presence of Dyslexia may well be the tip of an iceberg which may be masking much greater underlying problems.

Once we look at Dyslexia, as defined in its broadest sense (as in this book), then it becomes apparent that we may have to change our perspective of Dyslexia. It would seem that at least some of the different forms of Dyslexia are likely to be reflections of the presence of

 Reading a book, whilst lying in the bath eating a delicious hot cross bun, is one of the most relaxing activities that the author knows. For far too many students reading is not a relaxing hobby; instead it is a demanding chore.

**During the twenty-first century a different perspective
on Dyslexia is likely to evolve.**
Research will change our understanding of Dyslexia and so the
meaning of the term 'Dyslexia' will gradually alter.

different SpLD Profile conditions (and combinations thereof). It therefore seems highly likely that in many cases Dyslexia is an outcome of the presence of other medical conditions rather than being itself the cause of literacy difficulties. This can be the case when phonological difficulties are the basis of the Dyslexia, for such difficulties can be seen because of the presence of Articulatory Dyspraxia and Central Auditory Processing Disorder – especially the Auditory Decoding Deficit form of it. Central Auditory Processing Disorder would not have been named as the causal condition in the past as it was (and still is) a little-known condition in the UK although now many audiologists have become aware of it.

As this century progresses research, discussion and new ways of looking at Dyslexia will emerge and so our perspective of Dyslexia will change and no doubt countless controversies will exist as to exactly what the term means. Each person who looks at the student has an interest in a particular outcome and in a particular definition. Each party has different pressures and constraints affecting the way that they work and the way that they view Dyslexia. The parent wants adequate provision and support for his/her child. The student wants to be less frustrated, stressed and unhappy because of his/her difficulties and be able to show his/her knowledge with greater ease. The teacher would like an easy way to provide effective support and provision that will not use up a great deal of his/her valuable time and resources. In the UK's climate of 'payment by results' s/he also wants to enable the student to reach his/her potential. The LEA wants to achieve good results in the government's 'league tables' and to enable its students to achieve their potential in the most cost-effective way. The assessor wants to be able to accurately diagnose the student's literacy difficulties, identify the other conditions which are present and provide good advice on remediation strategies and resources. (Whether s/he works in the private or state sector will determine how much time can be allocated to the assessment and the writing of the report and can even affect the terms that can be used within it.)

Given the range of interests of the different parties it is not surprising that the 1999 report entitled 'Dyslexia, Literacy and Psychological Assessment' (ISBN 1 85433 310 0) was welcomed by some and greeted with concern by others. This report was written by a working party of the Division of Educational and Child Psychology of the British Psychological Society (Tel: 0116 254 9568). It looked at various aspects of Dyslexia; e.g. common usage of the term, early years' assessment and how the severity and persistence of literacy difficulties might be assessed. Based upon current knowledge and research it suggested that a phonological basis was the strongest explanation for Dyslexia although this was not the only cause and future research may emphasis other aspects of literacy functioning. *[Phonological skills relate to the student's ability to identify words automatically and the ability to encode (build words up from their sounds; e.g. c-a-t) and decode (break words down into their sounds and work out the word that the sounds represent.]* The report adopted the following 'working definition' of Dyslexia which describes the literacy difficulty but which does not include an explanation of its cause.

"Dyslexia is evident when accurate and fluent word reading and/or spelling develops very incompletely or with great difficulty. This focuses on literacy learning at the 'word level' and implies that the problem is severe and persistent despite appropriate learning opportunities. It

An effective assessment for literacy difficulties requires that assessors are allowed the time necessary to identify/diagnosing the range of conditions present at each assessment and that they have the ability to identify/diagnose the wide range of SpLD Profile conditions.

provides the basis for a staged process of assessment through teaching." (page 64)

The report goes on to say that "In terms of the UK's National Literacy Strategy, dyslexia can be defined as marked and persistent problems at the word level of the NLS curricular framework." (page 64) [*Thus, if a parent/teacher realises that the child is having difficulties in coping with the National Literacy word level work then pupil observation/change of teaching strategy is necessary leading to identification for, and then assessment of, Dyslexia. A similar route leading to assessment will need to be taken if any of the other difficulties mentioned in this book are noted.*]

There is a danger that this 'working definition' may be misunderstood and the terminology (words/phrases) within it be used in arguments about provision. This was not the intention of the working party of the Division of Educational and Child Psychology. They used the 'working definition' as a starting point to develop an understanding of the different theoretical explanations and research findings relating to Dyslexia. Thus, it is a starting point for assessment, not a self-limiting definition of Dyslexia. It is realised by all concerned that in each case a full picture of the whole student and his/her learning environment is required, including his/her strengths and weaknesses, and that his/her particular needs in all areas need to be considered.

When Dyslexia is present we will need to be aware, when looking at the student's literacy functioning, of both the broader and the narrower definitions of the condition if we are adequately to help him/her. If we do not do this then difficulties in areas such as reading comprehension, language, near-vision dysfunctioning etc. may be ignored. Both types of definition are based upon the understanding that we have also to look further afield and consider many other aspects of the student's functioning; e.g. that stress and anxiety affect working memory and so are likely to affect phonological working memory. Therefore, unless we look at the student as 'a whole' (and allow extra assessment/support time in order to achieve this) the help that the student receives is likely to be inadequate and inefficient.

As our knowledge increases so the definition of Dyslexia will continue to alter subtly throughout the twenty-first century. In the future we may start to regard Dyslexia as the descriptive term that describes the learning difficulty (rather than being the cause of the learning difficulty) and new terms may emerge. Thus, if assessors decide to adopt the working definition of The British Psychological Society's report when dealing with children then they may choose to describe literacy difficulties that fit the 'working definition' as 'Developmental Dyslexia' or 'Acquired Dyslexia'. All other forms of Dyslexia might then be described as 'Secondary Developmental Dyslexia', 'Secondary Acquired Dyslexia' or as 'literacy difficulties caused by the presence of the Specific Learning Difficulties/Dyslexia Profile'.

ENABLING THE STUDENT TO SUCCEED
Inappropriate provision can be very ineffective and very costly (both in financial and emotional terms). It may also achieve little except for such students losing faith in both their own abilities and in the ability of their educators to help them. A good example of this was the case of the primary school child who could still only read a few words after considerable input from special needs' staff. It appeared that no-one had thought to ask him whether he

was reading the 'black or the white bits' on the page. Since he had been trying to read the 'white bits' it was not surprising that the special needs support that he was receiving was ineffective. (See page 30 for further information on this difficulty.)

> **Throughout the student's education it is vital that we look at the overall impact of the student's range of difficulties. The presence of a number of low-level difficulties can have as great an impact as the presence of one condition which is severe.**

The acquisition of literacy skills is the route by which we are enabled to show our knowledge and through these skills (especially those of written recording) we can achieve our academic and life goals. Literacy provision tends to concentrate on reading and spelling skills but the ability to record one's own thoughts (and show knowledge) is, therefore, of equal importance. The presence of any of the conditions found within (or associated with) the SpLD Profile can cause the student to go into an 'overload' situation when handwriting text. This difficulty is especially noticeable when any combination of Dyslexia, Graphomotor Dyspraxia and a language impairment are present. (The 'overload' is caused by the effort of working out what to say, whilst planning and constructing the sentence, and simultaneously spelling the words correctly and writing the sentence legibly.) As a result of the student's difficulties s/he may severely under-perform in written tasks especially in English and this can cause students to have major problems in showing their knowledge when writing.

Teachers may spend a good deal of time 'brain storming' ideas about a particular topic and produce a good task sheet, which provides well-thought-out advice on how the task should be completed. However, it is not always realised that some students may need to be trained in how they can 'make the text flow' from one sentence to another (and from one paragraph to another). The greater the language difficulty the more difficult such tasks are, especially if sentence construction is one of the main difficulties present.

 Sentence-construction difficulties and difficulties in planning, organising and prioritising information can cause students to have considerable problems in putting their thoughts on paper.

Case Study – Male GCSE student
This student's handwriting was slow and letters were often not joined, both language difficulties and Dyslexia were present. This pattern of difficulties caused him to be in an 'overload' situation when writing and to have difficulties with sentence construction. As part of his GCSE work he was asked to compare two pictures. He had plenty of ideas but tended to provide only 'bits' of information via short phrases both orally and in writing; though some of his phrases showed that he possessed a reasonably good vocabulary. He used this way of providing information partly because he knew that the teacher knew what the picture looked like (so therefore he did not see the need to explain the picture in depth). He also did not know the words/phrases to use to connect the phrases/sentences together, and the words that would be expected to go together; e.g. the picture <u>shows</u>, the image <u>reveals</u>. The latter problem was partly because he thought that he needed to include a more complex word than 'shows' (so was trying to work out what word the teacher wanted and to access it from memory). The problem also occurred because, like many boys where Dyslexia is present, he only read material that he had to read for school and so did not have enough experience of written language. His low-level language difficulties also meant that his oral use of language was limited. Females tend to be more verbal than males and boys can be quite brief when using language even when no language impairment is present! So, when language

impairment is present the boy who speaks in short phrases and single-word answers is at a disadvantage when it comes to writing sentences. Sentence construction had always been a weak point for this student (at age twelve he had not known what made up a sentence). The appropriate use of a group of relevant words was discussed with him as an aid to improving his sentence construction so making his written work more fluent; e.g.

- the theme/idea/concept 'carries on', 'is continued in'
- the 'words/copy 'tells us', 'informs us', 'explains'.

By the time the student approaches the GCSE years changes in provision will be necessary. The focus must move from basic reading, spelling and handwriting skills to enabling the student to achieve the necessary grades which in turn enable him/her to go onto the next stage of education/achieve his/her career goals. Many SpLD Profile students are likely to need extra tuition in understanding examination questions and in the use of any extra examination time that they are given because of their difficulties. Coursework assignments can provide about 20% (or more in some subjects) of the final GCSE grade. Therefore, when students are in an 'overload' situation when writing it is best to provide them with an amanuensis for assignment coursework (someone who writes for him/her). Alternatively, they can use a voice-activated dictation program for such work; e.g. Dragon Naturally Speaking Mobile (Tel: 01242 678575). Some students may find that just the use of a predictive lexicon reduces the overload enough (see page A33 for details). These strategies can also be used for vocational courses both for coursework and to aid the development of written-work skills.

During the second year of a GCSE (or final part of a vocational) course a decision has to be made as to whether the student needs (and is happy to use) such provision during the final examinations, or whether other strategies have to be found to enable the student to produce a reasonable standard of written work. (Note: examination dispensations need to be applied for early, see page A8.) Various strategies are likely to be needed at this stage. Most students will need to use a planning tool which suits their learning style (see 'Planning and Organisation Solutions', page A33). Some students prefer to hand-write their answers. Such students may need to be trained to write on alternate lines and then go through the text amending errors and adding descriptive words etc. (The writing on alternate lines gives the student the room s/he needs to make such alterations.)

Unless we refocus our help, and progress towards providing adequate and appropriate support for the older student, our work in teaching the student to read, spell etc. in the early years may have achieved little in enabling him/her to go on to the career of his/her choice. Unfortunately the loss of self-esteem, when poor results are obtained in external examinations, can carry on right through adulthood. The use of strategies such as those mentioned above can result in the student obtaining an overall 'C' grade through gaining 'A' and 'B' grades for assignment work and a 'D' grade in the examination. It is this 'C' grade that opens to the door to further education colleges. (According to the course that the student wants to take s/he will usually need four or five 'C' grades at GCSE level to enter a course.)

 We need to continually monitor where the student is on the 'path to success'. As we approach the GCSE years we need to refocus our provision from the basic literacy skills to those skills needed in order to gain the external examinations that enable the student to achieve his/her life goals.

Appropriate and cost-effective support (no matter what the age of the student) can only occur if all of those involved with him/her can recognise all of the conditions mentioned within this book. Understanding that there is likely to be at least one underlying condition present when the term Dyslexia is used is important, for not only will we need to provide for the Dyslexia but we will also need to provide remediation strategies/support for the other conditions which are present. It means that if we are to meet the needs of the student then we will need to adjust our methods and the learning/work/home environment to suit the person when any of the Specific Learning Difficulties Profile conditions are present. This knowledge enables us to realise that our teaching of literacy skills is likely to be ineffective, unless prior to starting remediation, we work out the combination of SpLD Profile conditions which are present.

The 'Solutions for Specific Learning Difficulties: Identification Guide' enables the reader to recognise the conditions associated with the term 'The SpLD Profile'. The role of 'Literacy Solutions' is to enable the reader to set the student on the path to obtaining success. However, we have not finished teaching literacy skills to our SpLD Profile students until we have progressed to moving the focus of provision beyond the basic skills and onto the higher skills needed to enable them to obtain success in life and academic goals. The final book in the 'Finding the Key to Specific Learning Difficulties' series ('Successful Strategies for Specific Learning Difficulties', ISBN 1 901544 67 2) shows how we can enable students to reach the 'end of the path' and so achieve their goals.

 No-one would expect a wheelchair-bound person to climb Mount Everest without support. In the same way, when the SpLD Profile is present, we cannot expect the student to succeed in climbing learning and behavioural mountains on a daily basis.

TOGETHER WE CAN ACHIEVE SUCCESS

We can enable our students to climb their literacy mountains. If we gain the necessary knowledge and experience we can help these students to find ways to tunnel through their 'mountains' and find the 'mountain passes' that reduce the task to more manageable proportions. The more we enable them to achieve, the greater our own reward as we share their delight in their successes, no matter how great or small. Only by co-operating with each other can we provide the support that such students need. The student is one part of a team. The team consists of the person and his/her network (family, friends, classmates, professionals and the adult student's work colleagues). In order to achieve the person's goals each element of this team needs to work together and support each other.

Thus, we have found the 'key to success' once we:
- know the conditions which are present
- start to remediate the underlying dysfunctions
- teach the student using strategies that can work (given the combination of the underlying conditions and the student's natural learning style)
- reduce the student's workload (whilst still keeping the level of work in-line with his/her intellectual functioning)
- reduce the student's stress
- praise the student in appropriate ways
- adjust the task, our teaching strategies, our teaching resources and the environment to enable the student to achieve the task
- provide appropriate support, so enabling the student to show his/her knowledge
- work co-operatively with each other

This book has been written to enable the reader 'to find the key' and so achieve successful literacy teaching.

Appendix 1 – Main sources of help and support

If you live in a country other than the UK then contact the relevant UK agency and they should be able to supply you with the contact details of your country's organisation.

DYSLEXIA

All of these organisations provide information; the first three provide conferences & telephone support as well.

The British Dyslexia Association 98 London Road, Reading, United Kingdom RG1 5AU Tel: 0118 966 2677 Fax: 01734 351 927 Helpline: 0118 966 8271 website http://www.bda-dyslexia.org.uk

Scottish Dyslexia Association Unit 3, Stirling Business Centre, Wellgreen Place, Stirling, Scotland, FK8 2DZ Tel: 01786 446650

Adult Dyslexia Organisation 336 Brixton Road, London, SW9 7AA Tel: Helpline: 020 7924 9559, Adminstration: 020 7737 7646 Fax: 020 7274 7840

Real & Effective Action for Dyslexia Chairperson: Mrs Gillian Cloke, 21 Mylady's Mile, Hollywood, Co. Down, Northern Ireland, BT18 9EW

The following organisations provide lessons for students & training for teachers. Ring the BDA for details of local centres.

The Dyslexia Institute 133 Gresham Road, Staines, TW18 2AJ Tel: 01784 463851 website: www.dyslexia-inst.org.uk Has many training centres throughout the UK and produces a very informative journal – 'Dyslexia Review'.

The Hornsby International Dyslexia Centre Glenshee Lodge, 261 Trinity Road, London, SW18 3SN Tel: 020 8874 1844

Helen Arkell Dyslexia Centre Frensham, Farnham, Surrey GU10 3BW Tel: 01252 792 400

Dyslexia Unit, University of Wales Bangor, Gwynedd, LL57 2DG Tel: 01248 383841

DYSPRAXIA

These organisations provide conferences, information & telephone support.

Dyspraxia Foundation 8 West Alley, Hitchin, Herts, United Kingdom, SG5 1EG Tel: 01462 454 986 Fax: 01462 455 052 Publishes 'Praxis II'.

Dyspraxia Foundation Adult Support Group Contact: Mary Colley, 7 Sumatra Road, London, NW6 1PS Tel: 020 7435 5443 Provides conferences, information, support.

The Dyspraxia Association Contact: Aileen Tierney, Chairperson, The Dyspraxia Association, 5 Blackglen Court, Sandyford, Dublin 18 Tel: 01 295 7125

The following organisation provides assessment and a remediation programme

The Dyscovery Centre 12 Cathedral Road, Cardiff, CF1 9LJ Tel: 01222 788666

AUTISTIC SPECTRUM DISORDER

The National Autistic Society 393 City Road, London, EC1V 1NE Tel: 020 7833 2299 Fax: 0171 833 9666 website: www. oneworld.org/autism_uk Provides conferences, in-service training & support.

Scottish Society for Autistic Children Hilton House, Alloa Business Park, Whins Road, Alloa, FK10 3SA

LANGUAGE

AFASIC – Association for all Speech Impaired Children 69-85 Old Street, London EC1V 9HX Tel: 020 7841 8900 Holds conferences, provides information sheets and booklets plus has a helpline.

Royal College of Speech and Language Therapists 7 Bath Place, Rivington Street, London, EC2A 3DR Tel: 020 7613 3855

ICAN Barbican Citygate, 1-3 Dufferin Street, London, EC1Y 9NH Provides information/publications on communication difficulties.

National Association of Professionals concerned with Language Impairment in Children (NAPLIC) Contact: A Reevey, 14 Heritage Close, Peasedown St. John, Bath, BA2 8TJ A multidisciplinary organisation. Holds conferences & provides information.

CFS/ME

ME Association Stanhope House, High Street, Stanford-le-Hope, Essex, SS17 0HA Tel: 01375 642466

Action for ME P.O. Box 1302, Wells, BA5 2WE Tel: 01749 670799

Action for Young ME www.ayme.org.uk

ATTENTION DEFICITS
The ADHD Family Support Group UK
c/o Mrs G Mead, 1A High St, Dilton Marsh, Westbury, Wiltshire, BA13 4DL
Tel: 01373 826 045 Fax: 01373 825 158. Has free ADD/ADHD information pack.
The Hyperactive Children's Support Group 71 Whyke Lane, Chichester, West Sussex, PO19 2LD. Tel/Fax: 01903 725182
Provides a Basic Introductory Pack.
ADDISS, PO Box 340, Middlesex, HA8 9HL Tel: 0208 905 2013 Fax: 0208 386 6466. Stocks a wide range of ADD/ADHD books & holds national conferences.

OSTEOPATHY
Osteopathic Centre for Children
Harcourt House, Cavendish Square, London. Tel: 020 7495 1231 Fax: 020 74951232
General Council and Register of Osteopaths 56 London Street, Reading, RG1 4SQ Tel: 01734 576585

TWINS
Twins And Multiple Birth Association
17 Clevedon Green, South Littleton, Evesham, Worcestershire, WR11 5TY

HOMEOPATHY
Can be helpful in some cases especially with regard to stress, behaviour and poor sleep.
The Society of Homeopaths 2 Artizan Road, Northampton, NN1 4AU
Tel: 01604 21400 Fax: 01604 22622

VISUAL & PERCEPTUAL DIFFICULTIES
College of Optometrists 43 Craven Street, London, WC2N 5NG Tel: 020 7839 6000
Institute of Optometry 56-62 Newington Causeway, London SE1 6DS Tel: 020 7407 4183
The Irlen Institute (International contact: Patricia Clayton, Irlen Centre, 123 High Street, Chard, Somerset, TA20 1QT Tel/Fax: 01460 65555
British Association of behavioural optometrists (BABO) 72 High Street, Billericay, Essex CM12 9BS Tel: 01277 624 916 www.behaviouraloptometry.com
Behavioural Optometrists specialise in visually-related learning difficulties.

New Scientist
151 Wardour Street, London, W1V 4BN. Website: www.newscientist.co.uk Their reader service is Tel: 020 7331 2702. The back edition of New Scientist of 24th April 1999 mentioned in this book is available from John Denton's Tel: 020 8503 0588.

CHILDHOOD HEMIPLEGIA AND ASSOCIATED CONDITIONS
Hemihelp 166 Boundaries Road, London, SW12 8EG Tel: 020 8672 3179
Offers help regarding Childhood Hemiplegia to parents and professionals. Produces a newsletter. Helpline: Monday – Friday 10am – 1pm.
Child Head Injury Trust Mrs Sue Colville (secretary), The Children's Head Injury Trust, c/o Neurosurgery Department, The Radcliffe Infirmary, Woodstock Road, Oxford, OX2 6HE

OTHER ORGANISATIONS
PATOSS (Professional Association of Teachers of Students with Specific Learning Difficulties) PO Box 66, Cheltenham, Gloucestershire, GL53 9YF
Membership is open to teachers and other professionals.
Handwriting Interest Group Details of membership: Felicity Barnes, 6 Fyfield Road, Ongar, Essex, CM5 0AH
Institute of Neuro-Physiological Psychology Warwick House, 4 Stanley Place, Chester. Tel: 01244 311414
Provides training for Neuro-Developmental Delay.
NASEN (National Association for Special Educational Needs) NASEN House, 4/5 Amber Business Village, Amber Close, Amington, Tamworth, Staffs., B77 4RP Tel: 01827 311500. Produce a wide range of useful books & hold conferences. They publish three journals 'British Journal of Special Education', 'Support for Learning' and 'Special'. Membership is open to professionals, parents etc..

Appendix 2 – Teaching Methods

Tips for teaching reading, spelling and writing patterns using cumulative, structured multisensory teaching techniques

The following teaching method is usually recommended for a person with a Specific Learning Difficulty in Literacy:

- All sound patterns taught must be based against all previously learnt patterns.

- Never assume that anything has been learnt until the individual is able to correctly read/ spell the sound pattern etc. on a regular basis for several months!

- Only one new pattern is introduced at a time; e.g. you cannot introduce the word 'spring' until 'sp', 'ing' and finally 'spr' have been introduced.

Each sound pattern is a link in the chain of memory

- The vowels are attached to each new consonant blend; thus if 'ing' is taught then follow it immediately by 'ang', 'ung' and 'ong'.

- Teach final sound patterns first; e.g. the ones that appear at the end of the word. Just put a single consonant in front of the ending e.g. when teaching 'at' teaching the words 'bat', 'cat' and 'hat' is okay but not 'sprat' unless 'spr' has already been both taught **and learnt.**

Use the Phonic Alphabet inside the front cover (or design a similar one with the student based on his/her interests) so that the student knows automatically the basic sounds that individual letters represent and the names of the letters. The instructions for using this alphabet are on the inside back cover.

Use methods which involve the use of at least three senses simultaneously; e.g. say the word (and/or its component sounds) whilst looking at it and writing it. (Some students will not be able to use this many senses together and/or they will find it much easier to learn if one sense in particular is not used. See Chapters 2 and 8 for further details.)

Connect every new sound pattern to previously taught ones; e.g.
- "Last week we looked at 'it'".
- Ask the individual to say the sounds of the two letters in the word 'it'.
- "Now if we take off the 't' and add 'p' what will we get?" (The answer should be 'ip'.)

Then do this with words such as:
- 'nit' becomes 'nip'   'kit' becomes 'kip'   'sit' becomes 'sip'

If the individual is not able to do this then s/he needs phonological awareness training via schemes such as Sound Linkage by Hatcher, and progress is likely to be slow until such training is given.

Remediation lessons

Use between 50% and 75% of each lesson for revision of previously taught work. If the student has severe difficulties 90% revision may be necessary.

Class lessons

Continuous revision enables the student to forget less and can help him/her connect information. It can be achieved via homework tasks and through 5–10 minutes revision of previous work at the beginning of each lesson. Revision at the end of a lesson helps achieve a better level of learning. It can occur via the teacher leading a class discussion whilst creating a pictorial record (e.g. chart, Mind Map). The chart etc. can then be put on the wall as a continuous reminder of the work.

The Amended Fernald Method

1 Take a piece of A4 paper.

2 Put it so that the long side is at the bottom.

3 Fold it into three sections as shown below. The top section is for the top parts of letters like 'd' and 'l' (the ascenders), the middle part is for letters which are the same height as 'x' and the bottom part is for the descenders (the bottom parts or 'tails' of letters such as 'g').

4 Write a word on the piece of paper in joined writing using the type of writing model that the student has to use at school. The word should be written using thick wax crayon or a broad felt tip.

5 Write words that fit the same sound pattern in both joined and printed writing in the top left-hand corner. Put a picture there to help the student remember the pattern.

6 The adult says the word, the student says the word.

7 The student says the sound of each letter or sound blend as s/he writes them (the adult should guide the student's hand if necessary as the idea is for the student to write over the writing on the sheet in fluid strokes. If the word is more than four letters long then the student should write the word so that s/he lifts his/her hand off the page at the end of a sound blend.

8 The adult says the word, the student says the word.

9 Repeat from 6 – 8 at least 5 times.

10 Using lined paper the student reads and then writes the word from memory.

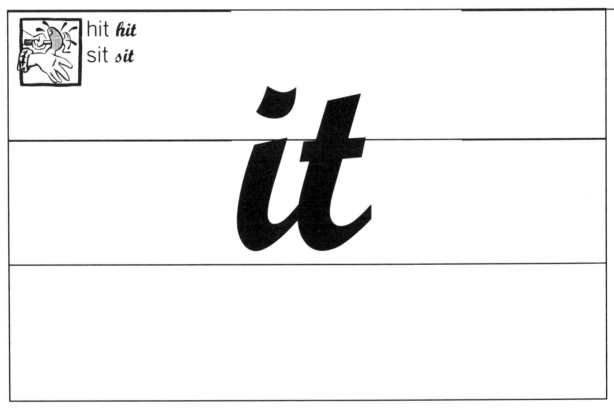

Notes:
- When Dyspraxia is present the student may dislike the feel of the text produced by the wax. Such students should trace the word with their finger and/or write the word in the air first and then trace over it with their own writing tool.

Acknowledgement: Stephanie Dart for the idea for an Amended Fernald card.

A4

ALTERNATIVE TEACHING METHODS

Any combination of these methods can be used alongside or as an alternative to multisensory methods. In the latter case they are used when the combination of SpLD Profile conditions that are present make multisensory methods less effective.

Method 1. Learning to read contextually

This method is very useful when any form of Dyslexia is present. It has been found to be an effective strategy when both phonological and Occulomotor Delay/Dyspraxia are present. The student is given a group of flash cards (maximum ten cards) of words that s/he knows. (If at all possible the words should all follow the same sound pattern; e.g. 'art', 'cart'; etc. They should also have, whenever possible, a picture illustrating the word.) The student puts two of the cards on the desk and then orally constructs a sentence using the two words:

- As s/he says the word in the sentence s/he must point to the appropriate card.
- The tutor listens out for any new words the student introduces which belong to the same sound pattern. These new words are written on flash cards which are then introduced one at a time into the pack of flash cards.
- The tutor should tape-record the student's sentences and write questions using the flash card words that reflect the words used by the student in sentences; e.g. if the flash card words are: 'sea' and 'tea' then the student might say, "I go to the sea cadets after tea". The tutor then would type a sentence such as: "When do you go to the sea cadets?" These questions would then be answered by the student (either hand-written or using the computer depending upon whether handwriting difficulties are present etc.) as a reinforcement task.

As the student will know the topics being mentioned in the questions s/he will be able to make better guesses as to the unknown words in the sentences. Better guessing and the frequent re-reading of known words .. improves reading ability and confidence. A

natural follow-up to the 'ea' pattern in this case would be the 'et' pattern (cadet, pet, set).

Method 2. Learning to read by association

The student should construct a Mind Map of a particular sound pattern using the words that s/he has just covered in Activity 1. Discussion should take place regarding other words that s/he could add to the Mind Map and other connections s/he could make; e.g. if the central theme is 'art' words s/he could have one branch which explores other 'vowel-rt' words; e.g. 'curt', 'hurt'. As each branch is colour-coded the colours will visually help the memory of the pattern. The same idea of colour-coding can be used on the flash cards.

Method 3. New words/words s/he finds difficult to remember

Do the following in the order shown:

1. Draw the word on the floor and walk him/her round the word (keeping him/her facing the front at all times; e.g. to construct the letter 'c' s/he takes two sideways steps to the left, two steps backwards and two sideways steps to the right).
2. Use the Amended Fernald Method (found on the previous page).
3. The adult should draw on the student's back the word that s/he has just walked round and another word which has a very different shape. See if s/he can recognise the one that s/he walked round. (Note: When Developmental Dyspraxia is present students may not recognise that they have been touched on the back and may think that they have been touched on another part of the body; e.g. the thigh. It is therefore better in the school situation for the tutor to write the word on the back of the student's hand instead.
4. Use the Amended Fernald method once more.

Method 4: Learning to read through personalised Phonic Stories

This method can be used with or without a computer. It is best to use the computer if the student has difficulties with handwriting (or finds handwriting frustrating as can occur when ADD is present) as it puts the student under much less pressure.

If the student is a child then, as long as s/he will work with a parent, all of the reinforcement of this activity can take place at home. Each story will take between 20-30 minutes for the student to type. This method trains visual memory and mainly teaches the student to read but usually improves spelling too. It can be very effective when Occulomotor Delay/ Dyspraxia and/or phonological difficulties are present.

It is recommended that these story lessons are given at least three times a week. A group of fifty of these lessons should give his/her reading the impetus that s/he needs to progress, though improvement should be noted long before that.

A. Using, whenever possible, the sentences that the student spoke in Method 1 design personalised four-sentence stories which cover one sound pattern and which contain the student's name or items relevant to him/ her (pets, family members etc.); e.g.

- After tea John went to the sea cadets.
- They went to the beach.
- The water had breached the bank.
- The sea had come in.

B. Each sentence should be divided into phrases of no more than four words; e.g.
After tea   John went   to the sea cadets.
Each phrase should be written/typed in large letters on a strip of paper.
C. The student is shown the first phrase and the tutor reads the words (pointing at each one as s/he says it).
D. The student is then shown the phrase for a few seconds. S/he types what s/he remembers. (S/he can ask to see the strip of paper as many times as s/he wishes.)
E. Once the story is completed s/he reads it

out. A picture is computer-generated to go with the story (e.g. via clipart).
F. The picture and the text are printed out (preferably in colour).
Stories can include a maxium of three words that do not follow previously covered work but these words must be on show all the time and the student not be required to type them from memory.

Reinforcement activities
The story is read out loud to an adult by the student as follows:
Week 1: on a daily basis

Week 2: four times a week.
(During this week the student will work out with the adult the separate sounds within each word, say them; e.g. ca-det, and then underline each one.)

Week 3: three times a week

Week 4: twice a week

Week 5 onwards: once a week.

Weeks 2 – 4 every time s/he reads the story s/he will:
- Read the story
- Sound out all of the sound patterns
- Read the story again.

Method 5. Stile Dyslexia Cards (available from LDA)
These cards provide a mainly visual and movement method by which an understanding of phonic skills can be shown. They can be used both at home and in school to help support his/her phonological work.

Suitable software for reinforcing spelling
Helicop and Henrietta's book of spells (both suitable for PC's). These programs are fun ways of improving spellings which teach reading as well. Can enter your own word lists. Best to keep the word lists very small at the start (e.g. 5 words). Available from Rickitt Educational Media (Tel: 01458 253636).

BE FLEXIBLE
TEACH STUDENTS IN THE WAY THAT THEY CAN LEARN.

Appendix 3 – Training

 A number of readers may have become very interested in assisting SpLD Profile students and want to go on to further training. Various training opportunities are now available and at varying costs ranging from being free to £1000+. There are a variety of courses available throughout the country. Local Education Authorities, Medical authorities and many agencies run courses and conferences. Some courses are based on attendance only; others require you to pass an examination either by doing assignment and/or by an examination. Courses operate at different times of the day and some have weekend sessions. The prices vary from being free to very expensive and the amount you pay often does not reflect upon the quality of the speakers – the authoress has been to some brilliant conferences that cost less than £50 for the day. Local Education Authorities are beginning to offer certificated courses which are accredited to various Higher Education establishments. Various types of qualification exist; e.g.:

OCR Qualifications (formerly known as RSA) The RSA Examinations Board, Progress House, Westwood Way, Coventry, CV4 8HS Tel: 01203 470033 Fax: 01203 468080 will provide you with information on your nearest provider of the following courses. (OCR stands for Oxford, Cambridge and RSA Examinations Board.)

CERTIFICATE FOR LITERACY AND NUMERACY SUPPORT ASSISTANTS (CLANSA AWARD). This course if for Learning Support Assistants.

OCR DIPLOMA (OR CERTIFICATE) FOR TEACHERS OF LEARNERS WITH SPECIFIC LEARNING DIFFICULTIES.
The course is part-time for one year. Various professionals besides teachers can obtain this qualification. Steph Smith was the first Learning Support Assistant to gain the RSA Diploma qualification in 1995. (She is now an LEA Learning Support Advisor.)

POST-GRADUATE DIPLOMA, PROFESSIONAL STUDIES IN EDUCATION (DYSLEXIA) This is administered by the Dyslexia Institute and is validated by Kingston University. It is a one year part-time course offered at or near a Dyslexia Institute centre in the UK and in Luxembourg, comprising two consecutive 15 week modules (The 'Dyslexic Learner as an Individual' and 'The Dyslexic Learner in Context'). Attendance is needed on one day each week plus private study.

Entry qualifications:
Applicants are normally teachers who hold a DFEE (DES) number and have at least three years classroom experience. Speech Therapists and occasionally Occupational Therapists and Psychologists with at least three years relevant experience may also be accepted.

Courses available in: Bath, Bedford, Brussels, Crewe, Durham, Glasgow, London, Sheffield, Tonbridge, Windsor, Luxembourg.
All applications for this course should be addressed to: Training Office (Post-Graduate Diploma): The Dyslexia Institute, Lloyds Bank Chambers, 71/73 High Street, Stone, Staffs, ST15 8AD Tel: 01785 819497 Fax: 01785 811431

UNIVERSITY COLLEGE OF WALES, BANGOR FACULTY OF EDUCATION; CERTIFICATE OF FURTHER PROFESSIONAL STUDIES 'SPECIFIC LEARNING DIFFICULTIES' (DYSLEXIA)

A one year part-time course requiring attendance for five weekends (from 9 a.m. Saturday - 3.30 p.m. Sunday) during the academic year, plus availability for short sessions regarding teaching practice.

Applicants: qualified teachers with three years teaching experience, although in exceptional circumstances those with other qualifications may be admitted.
Enquires to: Mrs C Coker, School of Education, University of Wales, Bangor, Holyhead Road, Bangor, Gwynedd, LL57 2PX.

A MASTER OF EDUCATION/DIPLOMA IN EDUCATION COURSE

Candidates for the M.Ed. degree must complete four modules plus a dissertation. Candidates for the Diploma in Education must complete four modules. Lectures take place over 5 weekends during the academic year.

Applicants: qualified teachers (minimum of 2 years experience) and other professionals.
Enquires to: School of Education, University of Wales, Bangor, Normal Site, Bangor, Gwynedd, LL57 2PX Tel: 01248 382932/2934.

Other organisations also offer courses and the British Dyslexia Association (see Appendix 1) can provide the reader with up-to-date information on courses and their providers. They can also provide advice as to which of those qualifications are presently accepted by the Department of Education when applying for examination dispensations for students. Up to 1999 only holders of the RSA/OCR Diploma SpLD, or qualified educational psychologists, were able to do this but changes are afoot. Holders of other qualifications (who have received extra training in assessment) are expected to be included in this list from the year 2000.

No matter which route you take (conferences/lectures or training) the accessing of more information will create the knowledge-base and support structure upon which appropriate, and adequate provision, can be negotiated and implemented.

Note: When applying for examination dispensations the educational establishment has to observe the Joint Council for General Qualifications guidelines. New guidelines were published at the end of 1999 called 'Examinations and Assessment for GCSE & GCE – Regulations and Guidance relating to Candidates with Special Requirements 2000'. It is available from: the Joint Council for General Qualifications Tel: 01223 553425. These guidelines include the 'Specialist Teacher's Assessment Report' which is the form that teachers with the relevant qualifications can use to request special examination arrangements. If the student is taking non-GCSE examinations then one needs the Assessment in General National Vocational Qualifications – Provision for Candidates with Particular Requirements (Special Assessment Needs) book. This is available from OCR Customer Information Bureau Tel: 01203 470033. Various assessment materials are now favoured when conducting assessments with older teenagers/adults. A list of these tests can be found at the end of an article by Gill Backhouse in the Patoss Bulletin (May 1999) available from Patoss, PO Box 66, Cheltenham, Gloucestershire GL53 9YF.

Appendix 4

Visual and Visual-perceptual Photocopiable Resources

The pages in this appendix may be photocopied by the owner of this book for the use of his/her students/children who are affected or believed to be affected by visual difficulties which are causing problems in acquiring and using literacy skills.

Checklist for visual problems

(Circle the response you think best describes your child:

Symptom	Please circle..
	Never.........Always

Symptom		
Reading comprehension is good to begin with, but reduces rapidly as reading continues	1 2 3 4 5 6	
Complaints of sore eyes or headaches when reading or writing	1 2 3 4 5 6	
Complaints of blurred vision, or of words going 'fuzzy' or double - 'or swimming about on the page'	1 2 3 4 5 6	
Reading comprehension is not as good as IQ would predict	1 2 3 4 5 6	
Has difficulty keeping place or line on the page when reading, and needs to use a marker to help	1 2 3 4 5 6	
Maths is better than reading (apart from where reading questions is concerned)	1 2 3 4 5 6	
Letters are reversed (e.g. b/d), and order of letters is confused in words (e.g. was/saw)	1 2 3 4 5 6	
Has difficulties learning to spell, and errors tend to be phonetic in nature	1 2 3 4 5 6	
Has problems copying material from blackboards and OHP's	1 2 3 4 5 6	
Loses concentration easily, and is distracted a lot	1 2 3 4 5 6	

If the total score on this quiz comes to more than 15-20, then it is probable that your child needs a behavioural vision examination

EYE MOVEMENT ACTIVITIES
Make these activities as enjoyable as possible both for you and your child!

Important: Read the Guidance Notes on Page 4 before starting these activities.

Activity One – 'Watch my thumbs!'
The child should be either standing, or sitting on a stool without any back support, facing the helper, with good upright posture.

1   The helper should face the child, holding his/herthumbs up at the child's chin level, about twelve inches from the child, and about six inches apart.
2   The aim of the activity is for the child to look at one thumb, keeping their eyes on it (try drawing smiley faces on the thumbs!), and then to switch gaze, without moving their head, to the other thumb when it wiggles.
3   Swap back and forth, encouraging the child to keep their gaze on the thumb until they are aware of the other thumb wiggling!
4   For advanced work, try asking the child to talk, sing or hum at the same time - this encourages them to 'multitask', and for the eye work to become more automatic.

Note: The following two activities use a torch. When Autistic Spectrum Disorder is present the student may be so fascinated by the light produced by the torch that they have difficulties in doing the task. Such students may even try to 'blow the light out' as they have made such a strong connection between the concepts of light and heat!

Activity Two – 'Numbers are it!'
Prepare a series of postcards (or similar) each with a number written in large letters on it.

1   Stick the postcards on the wall, at random within an area about five feet *(1½ metres)* square.
2   The child stands or sits, as in activity one, about four feet *(1¼ metres)* from the wall holding a small torch.
3   When the helper calls out a number, s/he should find the number on the wall as quickly as possible, and shine the torch at it (or point).
4   Again it is important that the head remains still for this activity – try balancing a bean bag or something similar on the head.
5   You can also help develop sequencing skills by calling out several numbers and having the child move from one to another in sequence. Do ensure, however, that you do not exceed the child's abilities. There is a fine line between stretching the child and simply making the whole task something to fail at!

Activity Three – 'Follow that fly!'
Equipment needed: a wall or large vertical surface of about ten feet by five feet (a blackboard in the classroom may be used). Two small torches.

1   The child sits or stands as in activity one, about five feet (1½ metres) from the wall holding one of the torches.

2   The helper shines a torch on the wall and the child tries to keep his/her torch beam on top of the helper's torch-beam as it is slowly moved around the wall. Again ensure that the head is still!

Activity Four – 'Paper hopscotch'

For this activity, take a book containing plenty of print, of a size appropriate to the child's reading level. *Note: The child needs to know the names or sounds of the letters of the alphabet to do this task.*

1   The child holds the book, possibly whilst sitting at a table, so that s/he is about twelve inches from the text.
2   He should try to read aloud the first and last letters of each line, without using a finger or pointer to assist.
3   If possible, the letters should be read in a smooth rhythmic manner, possibly to a beat clapped out by the helper, or to a metronome (if you have one!).
4   Aim to keep going for about four minutes.
5   As the task becomes easier, try decreasing the size of print, or asking the child to slowly move the book around as s/he reads the letters – this is really quite hard!

Activity Five – 'What a lot of dots!'

1   Take a newspaper and a red felt pen and ask the child to place a dot inside every solid letter s/he can find (e.g. letters that enclose a bit of space such as o, a, d, b, p, q,) as quickly as s/he can.
2   Try doing this over about ten lines of print at a time.
3   You can time the child to introduce an element of competition to the task. However, be careful of doing this when either fine motor Dyspraxia or Attention Deficits are present. If you are timing it, try adding two second penalties for every missed letter! (T*his strategy may have a negative affect on Attention Deficit students.*)
4   Repeat the task with different text each time, and look for improvements – some children love to see their results plotted onto a graph so that they can see the changes more pictorially!

Note: If the student is being taught a particular letter sound at school the task could be to put a dot on each letter of that type found. If Dyspraxia is present the student may have difficulties in controlling the pen/pencil used for the task – felt tips glide well over the page but some students press so hard that they quickly break the point. The same can happen with wax crayons and coloured pencils. Using the pen to 'point' at the relevant letters or using pens with stronger points (such as 'fine liners') may be more effective.

Students with fine motor difficulties have problems with writing and controlling small objects/tools. Attention Deficits students may have delayed development in this respect. (Some of them may not sit still long enough to develop such skills!) These students may find it frustrating and distressing that they cannot achieve the task at speed. They can feel very insecure when doing such tasks and there is the possibility that Attention Deficits students become very angry when doing timed tasks.

Activity Six – 'Magnet mazes'

Whilst this activity needs some equipment, it is great fun, and well worth the effort! Get hold of two small magnets, and a piece of card, such as the side of a cereal packet.

Drawing the maze

You can draw the maze by taking two pencils and holding them together to draw two lines at the same time that are the same distance apart.

1 Now draw a simple maze on the card, including several nice curves and bends. Holding the card flat, with the maze design on the upper surface, place one magnet at the start of the maze, whilst the child holds the other magnet underneath the card, so that it is attracting the magnet on the top surface.

2 The child should now use the lower magnet to guide the upper magnet around the maze, without of course deviating from the path!

3 As before, encourage the eyes to follow the magnet, without either the whole body or head being involved.

Note: This activity may not be suitable for students when fine motor Dyspraxia is present as it requires a good deal of control of the magnet. Increasing the size of the magnets is likely to make the task easier and so will attaching a stick to the bottom magnet. When Dyspraxia is present the student is likely to benefit from sitting in a chair that provides plenty of support whilst doing this task.

Activity Seven – 'Stop that car!'

For this activity, use small toy cars or, if they are not available, try using marbles. You will also need a small plastic pot or cup, just big enough to fit over the toy car, or marble. The activity is best done on a smooth floor covering, rather than on carpet.

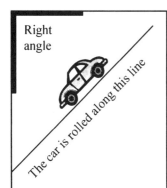

Right angle

The car is rolled along this line

To make the task harder, try drawing two lines about ten inches (25 centimetres) apart at right angles to the line of rolling, and make this the only area in which the cars/marbles can be 'caught' as they are rolled across it.

- The child should kneel on the floor, at right angles to the helper, who should be about three feet (1 metre) away.
- The helper rolls a car or a marble past the child, who must catch it with their cup. They get to keep the 'caught' ones, whilst the others live to roll another day!
- Again, encourage the child to use the eyes and not the head for the task.

Note: When gross motor (whole body movements) or fine motor Dyspraxia is present the student may find this task hard to achieve. If the child has difficulties in maintaining posture then do the task on the table with the child sitting in a chair which provides good support. If the child has spatial relationship difficulties/fine motor difficulties use a large cup (small plastic bucket) and a small car at first to make the task easier.

Activity Eight – 'Clock pointing'

- The child (whilst keeping his/her head still) points his/her finger with his/her arm outstretched at the top of the clock.
- His/her eyes focus on his/her finger and s/he follows it as s/he slowly moves it round the edge in a clockwise direction. This activity can be done using a bedroom window just before settling the child to sleep and on the way to school using the car windscreen.

GUIDANCE FOR USING THE EYE MOVEMENT ACTIVITIES SHEETS

THE ACTIVITIES ARE SUITABLE FOR HOME AND SCHOOL USE.

The exercises are designed to improve tracking, or eye movement work. We are not born with these skills but they develop as follows:

- The development of eye movements in children starts with the ability to maintain concentration on a target – e.g. the mothers face.
- Then follows the ability to move the eyes around and follow a target; doing this without having to involve the whole head and body in the movement is a subsequent and important step.

It is in these two areas of targeting and only moving the eyes that so many children get 'stuck', and do not develop efficient skills to cope. Bear this in mind when working on the following tasks, since it is desirable to overcome these traits where they are present. Try to gently encourage the child, without it becoming an issue that may lead to him/her becoming upset and losing faith in his/her ability to do the tasks. The Eye Movement Activities are simple activities that can be carried out at home, or in the classroom without fear of causing damage to the child's visual system.

Notes:

- Whilst there are many other areas that can be effectively trained at home, these should only be attempted under professional guidance, and are therefore not included here.

- **Do not do any form of training that involves covering an eye, or uses lenses or other devices that change sight, without expert advice.**

- There are many activities that can be used to stimulate eye movements, and those in Appendix 3 are merely starting points – often the best vision training tasks come from the child's own imagination, so be prepared to experiment!

- **Should the child become distressed at his/her performance however, then stop immediately. It may help to point out that difficulty with these tasks is NOT a sign of being 'thick', 'stupid', or anything else, but may be a good sign as to WHY the child is experiencing the difficulties they are having.**

  So often the fear of the unknown – not understanding why s/he cannot do what his/her peers can do - makes the problem seem so much worse, and anything you can do to help develop an understanding of what is happening can only be positive.

Exercises for the Remediation of Figure-Ground Visual-Perceptual Difficulties

Figure/ground perception

A student with difficulties in this area has difficulties in choosing which areas of a picture/ diagram s/he should concentrate upon; e.g. the foreground or the background. Overlapping objects may not be clearly perceived. The following examples are all computer-generated and can be simply extended by adding one more item to the number of shapes in any task. The tasks below should be done in the order 1–3. In each task there is an opportunity for the student to handle one of shapes. This can help the student to internalise the shape that s/he is looking at/being asked to reproduce.

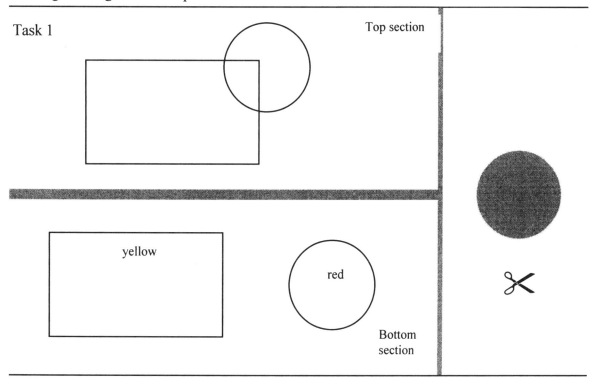

The student does the following:

Stage 1:

1. Using his/her finger the student traces round the outline of the rectangle in the bottom section and then in the top section.

2. Using his/her finger the student traces round the outline of the circle in the bottom section and then in the top section.

Stage 2:

3. An adult should cut out the circle marked with the pair of scissors and the student should stick it with blu-tack over the top of the circle in the diagram in the top section.

4. Using his/her finger the student should trace round the outline of the circle in the top section. Note: draw the student's attention to the 'feel' of the circle's edge as s/he traces.

5. The student should remove the circle and the blu-tack.

Stage 3:

6. The student should colour the rectangle in the top section yellow and the circle red. (Note: if the student uses wax/pencil crayons for this task s/he will have an orange section where the two shapes overlap and the adult should explain that red and yellow make orange.

Stage 4:

7. The adult should provide the student with two pieces of appropriately coloured clear acetate sheet cut into the same size and shape as the items in the bottom section.

8. The student places the items on top of one another until s/he creates the diagram in the top section.

Task 2

Stage 1

1. Take some phototgraphs of the student with one or two people (e.g. members of his/her family) or ask the family to provide such photos.

2. Ask the student to point to him/herself in each photo.

3. Make a reproduction of each photo (e.g. by colour photocopying them).

4. Cut out one of the heads of the people from the copies.

5. Ask the student to put the cut-out item onto the correct place on the original photos.

6. Put a clear (uncoloured) acetate sheet over an original photo and paperclip/blutack the photo and sheet together.

7. Give the student an OHP fine-nibbed pen. Ask him/her to draw round the outline of him/herself in the photo. (Then do the same task for any other particularly noticeable/easy outline items in the photo.)

Stage 2

Using simple pictures (or clipart from a computer) do the following:

1. Make two copies of the picture.

2. Cut one item out of one of the pictures; e.g. in the picture below, the paintbrush has been cut out. Ask the student to use his/her finger to trace round:

• the cut-out item on the left
• the cut-out item in the main picture.

3. Ask the student to place the cut-out item onto the right place in the main picture. Blu-tack the cut-out item into position. Ask the student to:

• use his/her finger to trace round the cut-out item in the main picture.
• remove the cut-out item from the main picture.

4. Put a clear (uncoloured) piece of acetate sheet on top of the main picture. Ask the student to trace round the cut-out item (in this case the paintbrush) in the main picture with an OHP pen.

Stage 3

Using the computer, re-colour the picture (this can be achieved in Microsoft Publisher by clicking on the picture and then pressing the right-hand mouse button.On the menu displayed go to Change Picture and then to Recolour Picture. Make the picture shades of grey and then repeat Stages 1– 2 above. *Note: the task can be varied by placing the cut-out item below, above and to the right of the main picture.*

Cut-out item   Main picture

Task 3

Give the student a cube to look at (e.g. a dice). Make sure that s/he knows that each face of a cube is called a 'square'. Get the student to hold the cube at different angles and to tell the adult what s/he notices as the angle at which it is held changes. Point to the cube in the top left-hand section of the diagram below. Ask the student to use his/her finger to trace the three shapes which make up the outline of the cube. In the same way the student then traces over the three shapes. Finally, the student has to point to the shape which s/he can also see in the cube. (Students with severe problems may need to have cut-outs of the three shapes which s/he lays over the appropriate part of the cube before s/he can be convinced as to which shapes are present.

A student with severe visual-perceptual difficulties may not realise how the representation of the cube has been made. In such cases the strategy of laying bits of straws along the edges of a large cube, joining them where they meet at the corners to create an open shape like the one below and holding the cube at different angles may be helpful.

Further tasks can be designed in the same way. The shapes should gradually become more complex.

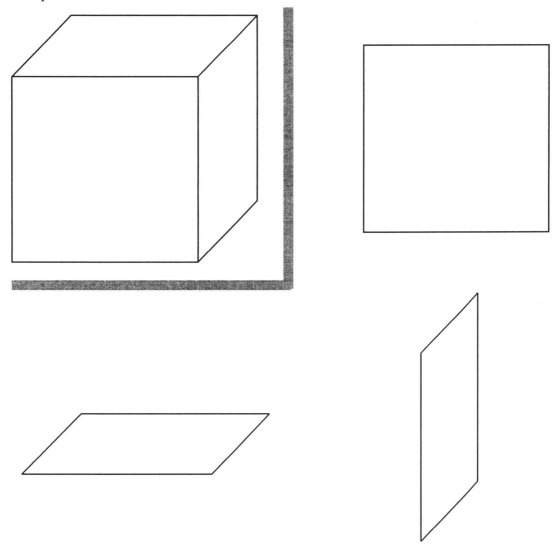

Task 4

The adult should make a copy (using thin cardboard) of the items on the left of the page.

1. The student should feel round the edges of the cardboard shape and show the adult which part is missing from the item on the right-hand of the page.

2. The student should use a finger to trace round the left-hand item and then using a pencil/pen etc. should complete the missing part of the right-hand item. If the student has difficulties in creating the correct angle (e.g. in the star) ask him/her to do the following:

- place the cardboard copy onto the right-hand shape
- ask him/her to use his/her finger to trace round the part that s/he has to draw 5 times
- draw the missing element on the right-hand item.

Note: Extend the task by creating different models using computer clipart/drawing the items and changing the position of the element that has to be completed; e.g. top, bottom, left, right, middle of the drawing.

Visual and Visual-Perceptual Distortions

The distortions in this section have been designed so that professionals/parents can gain a better understanding of the difficulties experienced by the student. They can also be used to identify that such distortions are occurring. Where the size of font makes the distortion look different both large and small font versions have been shown. Various distortions can occur. Instructions for using these sheets are on page A22.

1. Rivers of white: A double image of the words is causing areas of white to flow through the text.

leak. For them there has to be a compromi
n be achieved even with support. All too
far too late'!!! For all students the
fect many aspects of their lives both in an
instead we just learn strategies to overco
Solutions for Specific Learning Difficultie
5):

ts but assessment of that progress is not
e cope with higher literacy tasks simply
t has to make in order to achieve such tas
slexia shows that more of the brain is in u
ans a greater use of energy. Thus in an
need a reader because he has too high a
e exhaustion he faces in trying to do
exam the student may be functioning poor
t GCSE level can last for over a month
se, important that we do not just stop at

gave the cat the hat.

The rat saw the hat.   He w

asked the cat to give it to

hid the hat.   The rat found

put it on. He took the hat:

The cat chased the rat in t

that fell off the rat.   The ca

He took the hat to his ma

2. WHIRLPOOL EFFECT: Only the word/s in the centre of the whirlpool can be seen clearly.

The rat saw the hat.   He wan
asked to cat to give it to him
hid the hat.   The rat found th
put it on and stole it.

the rat in the hat.   The
'at.   The cat got the hat
the hat to his mat.   He
is head.   The cat in the

e hat. He wanted it. He
give it to him.   The cat
he rat found the hat. He
stole it.

d the rat in the hat. The
e rat. The cat got the hat
k the hat to his mat. He
his head. The cat in the

mat.

3. GLARE: Parts of the text are too dark and there are areas of light and dark text because the letters are overlapping horizontally or vertically. The overlap is vertical in this example.

4. OVERLAPPING TEXT: The text is far too dark throughout the page and a double image of each letter is seen.. Text can overlap vertically or horizontally.

DISAPPEARING TEXT: The ends of the words at the right-hand side appear to have fallen off the page and so cannot be seen.

The black cat sat on the red mat.
Along came a mouse with a hat. The
hat was too big for the mouse. The h
was just right for the mouse. The mouse
gave the cat the hat.

The rat saw the hat. He wanted it. He
asked to cat to give it to him. The ca
hid the hat. The rat found the hat. He
put it on and stole it.

The cat chased the rat in the hat. The
hat fell off the rat. The cat got the ha
again. He took the hat to his mat. He
put the hat on his head. The cat in the
hat sat on the mat.

Instructions for using the visual distortion sheets

Before showing the distortions to the student:
- Mask the page so that only one distortion is visible.
- Tell the student that s/he must not try to read the words. We are just going to find out if any of the things on these pages happen when s/he is looking at words. Always start with No. 5 to find out whether text does disappear off the page.
- Then show the student Visual Distortions 1– 4. Explain to the student that we only have part of a page and so we cannot see the ends of some words. Point to the particular part of the picture; e.g. the rivers of white running down the page and say, "Do you see this when you read". If the student says, "Yes" then ask him/her whether it happens all of the time, a little bit of the time, a lot of the time. (This gives the tutor an idea of the severity of the problem. Look at Chapter 7 for further details.)

Appendix 5
Useful Resources

The following symbols have been used to make it easier for you to choose suitable materials/ books. If the symbol appears by the heading for a particular subject group then all materials in that group are of the same level; e.g. see Memory group on this page. Unless otherwise stated all products can be read/used by all professionals, parents and other adults.

 EASY
These products are the easiest ones to use/read in a particular area.

 MIDDLE
The book is somewhere between easy and hard.

 The most difficult books in this group are indicated by half an apple.

 HARD
The mountain symbol. (It's a hard mountain to climb – but worth it when you get to the top!)

INDEX

MEMORY
All materials suitable for all ages.

MEMORY CARDS
(Published by Sutton Dyslexia Association, 21 Princes Avenue, Carshalton, Surrey, SM5 4NZ.) Consists of a pack of cards and a plastic wallet. Each card contains information on a particular area of difficulty of maths or literacy; e.g. confusing words, abbreviations etc. with the idea being that the student carries around with him/her cards relevant to his/her needs.

THE BASIC SKILLS AGENCY CARDS
(Published by The Basic Skills Agency, Commonwealth House, 1-19 New Oxford Street, London, WC1A 1NU) Similar in concept to the Memory Cards but in full colour and a little larger. Literacy-based cards include: The 35 most common words, when capital letters are used and a SMOG Ready Reckoner (which is very useful for teachers/parents to help work out the reading age of a particular book/article etc. The latter is also at the back of their booklet 'Making Reading Easier' which gives advice on how to make work sheets etc. easier to read.

MASTERING MEMORY (PC)
(Published by CALSC, Tel: 020 8642 4663) Computer program. Helps teachers to enable students of all ages to develop visual/ auditory memory skills and ultimately to develop strategies to improve their learning skills. Includes assessment. Also enables assessment of skills base.

Solutions for Specific Learning Difficulties: Identification Guide
by Jan Poustie et al
ISBN 1 901544 00 1

Recommended by:
The British Dyslexia Association, the Dyspraxia Foundation, ADDISS, the ADHD Family Support Group UK

This "easy-to-use and easy-to-follow"[1] book has been written in co-operation with thirty-nine specialists (including the main UK charities). It enables anyone to identify the various Specific Learning Difficulties which may be present.

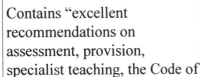

Contains "excellent recommendations on assessment, provision, specialist teaching, the Code of practice and much more."[2] It includes recommendations on how to make referrals, and information on the appropriate help and support agencies. (*1. Scottish Dyslexia Association 2. British Dyslexia Association's Contact magazine review 6/98.*)

Enables the reader to identify and refer, and put the first level of provision in for The Specific Learning Difficulties Profile including: Specific Language Impairment, Dyslexia, Near-vision dysfunctioning, mathematical difficulties (including Dyscalculia, handwriting difficulties, Central Auditory Processing Disorder, Autistic Spectrum Disorder Dyspraxia (including articulatory/verbal Dyspraxia and Occulomotor Dyspraxia), Attention Deficits (including Oppositional Defiant Disorder, Conduct Disorder, Attention Deficit Hyperactivity Disorder and Undifferentiated Attention Deficit Disorder)

It also has sections on:
- Assessment and Intervention (including the Code of Practice)
- Scotopic Sensitivity Irlen Syndrome
- Gaining Provision (from the professional's, parent's and child's point of view)
- Agencies who can provide help and support.

Music Solutions No. 1 Dyspraxia and learning to play a musical instrument
by Jan Poustie
ISBN 1 901544 55 9

This is the first book of its kind to be published in the UK. It explains how the different forms of Dyspraxia affect learning to play an instrument and suggests plenty of practical solutions to overcoming the difficulties. Includes:
1. The various forms of Dyspraxia
2. How each of the many aspects of Dyspraxia affect the acquisition of skills
3. Lessons & Teaching strategies
4. Speech & Language, Concerts, Tips
Also deals with some aspects of Dyslexia, Central Auditory Processing Disorder, Specific Language Impairment and Attention Deficits.

Practical Solutions for Specific Learning Difficulties: Life skills
by Jan Poustie
ISBN 1 901544 50 8

This comprehensive book shows how the different conditions affect the acquisition of the skills we need to live in our society. It provides practical solutions for some of the problems that can arise. Includes:
1. The Specific Learning Difficulties Profile, Communication skills
2. The intimate side of life
3. Measuring, Budgeting, Shopping, D.I.Y., Cooking, Childcare, Housework, Travel and Leisure
4. Skills needed for the workplace
5. Useful sources of information

ATTENTION DEFICITS

See Appendix 1 for help and support groups for this condition.

UNDERSTANDING ATTENTION DEFICIT DISORDER

A parent's guide to A.D.D. in children by Dr Christopher Green & Dr Kit Chee (ISBN 0 09 180844 8. Published by Vermilion, London). A very useful introduction to ADD for parents and professionals. Contains information on how to recognise ADD, practical advice, medication, sources of help and self-help for ADD adults.

ATTENTION DEFICIT/ HYPERACTIVITY DISORDER
- A practical guide for teachers

By Paul Cooper & Katherine Ideus (ISBN 1 85346 431 7. Published by David Fulton Publishers, London.) A clear and concise guide to classroom practice for teachers dealing with pupils who have this condition.

ALL ABOUT A.D.D.

By Mark Selikowitz (ISBN 0 19 553684 3 Published by Oxford University Press.) Provides comprehensive practical help for those with ADD and their families and the professionals who work with them.

YOU MEAN I'M NOT LAZY, STUPID OR CRAZY?!

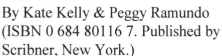

By Kate Kelly & Peggy Ramundo (ISBN 0 684 80116 7. Published by Scribner, New York.) One of the author's favourite books. This self-help book for adults contains a wealth of information and is fascinating to read. A book which should be read by all parents as they will then know more about how to avoid the pitfalls of adult ADD.

ADD IN ADULTS
Help for Adults Who Suffer from Attention Deficit Disorder

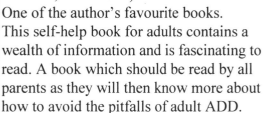

By Dr Gordon Serfontein (ISBN 0 7318 0390 6. Published by Simon & Schuster). A supportive and informative book for all people with ADD.

ANSWERS TO DISTRACTION

By Edward M Hallowell & John J Ratey (ISBN 0 671 52905 6. Publisher Simon & Schuster). This excellent audio tape explains Attention Deficit Disorder by answering commonly asked questions.

BEHAVIOUR & SELF ESTEEM

CRYING FOR HELP
The No Blame Approach to Bullying

By George Robinson & Barbara Maines (ISBN 1 873942 86 9. Published by Lucky Duck Publishing, Bristol.) A practical and down-to-earth approach to improving the lives of our students in the educational setting. A book that every school should have.

POSITIVE PUPIL BEHAVIOUR MANAGEMENT

By M Curry & C Bromfield (Published by East Devon Behaviour Support team, 97 Heavitree Rd, Exeter, EX1 2NE.) Provides positive behaviour management strategies for primary school teachers.

QUALITY CIRCLE TIME – in the primary classroom

By Jenny Mosley (ISBN 1 85503 229 5. Published by LDA, Duke Street, Wisbech, Cambs. PE13 2AE Tel: 01945 634 41.) This is a very good guide to ways of enhancing self-esteem, self-discipline and positive relationships.

STICKERS, CERTIFICATES, CROWNS, PRAISELETS

A large variety of these self-esteem boosters are available from LDA (Tel: 01945 463441). They also stock 'Home/school communication pads'.

AUTISTIC SPECTRUM DISORDER
See Appendix 1 for help and support groups for this condition.

THE WORLD OF THE AUTISTIC CHILD by Bryna Siegel (ISBN 0 19 507667 2. Publisher Oxford University Press.) Contains much information on recognition and aspects of the condition. Has a large section on classroom intervention strategies.

TEACHING CHILDREN WITH AUTISM TO MIND-READ – A PRACTICAL GUIDE by Patricia Howlin, Simon Baron-Cohen and Julie Hadwin (ISBN 0 471 97623 7. Publisher: John Wiley & Sons, Ltd. Chichester.) This easy-to-follow graded teaching guide provides practical guidelines, strategies and examples of teaching materials for helping children with Autistic Spectrum Conditions to improve their understanding of beliefs, emotions and pretence. It is suitable for professional and parental use.

AUTISM: A WORLD APART Narrated by Anna Massey (Available from: Hopeline Videos, PO Box 515, London, SW15 6LQ. This video shows the strain that autism places on the family and the difference that specialist education can make to enable those affected to lead happier and more fulfilled lives.

CHILDREN WITH AUTISM AND ASPERGER SYNDROME – A guide for practitioners and carers by Patricia Howlin (ISBN 0 471 98328 4. Published by John Wiley & Sons.) Provides practical ways of helping those affected by these conditions. Contains strategies for language impairments, social deficits and ritualistic and stereotyped behaviours. Includes outcomes of various treatments and case studies.

SOLVING BEHAVIOUR PROBLEMS IN AUTISM By Linda A Hodgdon (ISBN 0 9616786 2 3. Published by Quirk Roberts Publishing, USA. Suppliers: Mayer-Johnson or Cambridge Adaptive Communication – see next column for telephone numbers.) Very easy-to-understand & practical book.

THE AUTISTIC SPECTRUM - a guide for parents and professionals by Lorna Wing (ISBN 0 09 475160 9 Publisher Constable and Company Ltd., London.) Available from the National Autistic Society (see Appendix 1). An excellent comprehensive & practical guide for parents & professionals. Shows how people with autism experience the word, the reasons for their disturbed behaviour & resistance to change. Explains ways of teaching students.

AUTISTM AND ASPERGER SYNDROME Edited by Uta Frith (ISBN 0 52138608 X. Publisher Cambridge University Press, Cambridge, UK.) Contributors to this book: M Dewey, Uta Frith, C Gillbert, F Happé, D Tantam and Lorna Wing. Includes: the first ever translation of Asperger's paper, a look at the syndrome and its varied presentations which show how much adaptation, learning and personal development is possible if there is a sensitive understanding of the precise problems involved. Looks at the syndrome from childhood to adulthood.

BOARDMAKER (PC or MAC) Published by Mayer-Johnson Co. who originated the Picture Communication Symbols which are used in augmentative communication. Tel: 001 619 550 0084.Various UK distributors: Winslow Press (books only) Tel: 01869 244644, SEMERC (software) Tel: 0161 6274469, Cambridge Adaptive Communication (all products) Tel: 01223 264 244. Includes: various languages, 3000 Picture Communication Symbols & a drawing program through which displays can be created. Can add pictures/photos. The National Autistic Society stock a variety of titles including:
•Asperger Syndrome, a practical guide for teachers by Cummie, Leach & Stevenson
•Understanding and teaching children with autism by Jordan and Powell.
•Autism and learning: a guide to good practice by Jordan and Powell.

CHILDHOOD HEMIPLEGIA

Information on specific learning difficulties and childhood hemiplegia can be found in the following articles. Please note that they are very complex to read!

PSYCHOLOGICAL ASPECTS OF HEMIPLEGIA
by Robert Goodman
(From Archives of disease in childhood – March 1997, Vol 76, No. 3 pages 177-178 available from the BMJ publishing group, BMA House, Tavistock Square, London WC1H 9JR Tel: 0171 383 6305.)

IQ AND ITS PREDICTORS IN CHILDHOOD HEMIPLEGIA
by Robert Goodman and Carole Yude
(From Developmental Medicine and Child Neurology, 199638. 881-890.)

'THE PREVALENCE AND CORRELATES OF SPECIFIC LEARNING DIFFICULTIES IN A REPRESENTATIVE SAMPLE OF CHILDREN WITH HEMIPLEGIA'
by I Frampton, C Yude and R Goodman
(From the British Journal of Educational Psychology (1198)68, 39-51 published by The British Psychological Society.

NEURO-MATURATIONAL/DEVELOPMENTAL DELAY

BRAIN GYM – TEACHER'S EDITION
by P. & G. Dennison
(ISBN 0-942143-02-7).
Some of these exercises have been found to be useful by some students. This book can be used by either professionals, parents or affected adults. It provides both the exercises plus an explanation of what each exercise does. There are also Brain Gym books especially for parents.

A TEACHER'S WINDOW INTO THE CHILD'S MIND by Sally Goddard
(ISBN 0 9615332 5 0).
Explains how the different primitive and postural reflexes can affect learning. It suggests strategies and programmes that can be used inside and outside of the classroom.

VISUAL AND VISUAL-PERCEPTUAL DIFFICULTIES

READING BY THE COLOURS
by Helen Irlen
(ISBN 0 89529 482 6. Published by Avery Publishing Group.)
This book explains Scoptopic Sensitivity Irlen Syndrome (also known as Meares-Irlen Syndrom). It describes how the Irlen Method can improve reading skills.

VISUAL AIDS
A variety of these exist to help the student keep his/her place/see the words more clearly when reading; e.g. 'Linetracker' (Taskmaster Tel: 0116 270 4286) and the 'Dex Frame' (LDA Tel: 01945 463441 or Ruth McCarthy Tel: 01754 872 163).

ANN ARBOR MATERIALS
Age suitability: All
Level of ability: All

This publisher produces a wide range of photocopiable books which help with visual functioning including materials for literacy, numeracy and music. These are available from:
Ann Arbor Publishers Ltd, P.O. Box 1, Belford, Northumberland, NE70 7JX.

SPEECH, LANGUAGE AND LISTENING SKILLS
See Appendix 1 for help and support groups for this condition.

THE NUFFIELD CENTRE DYSPRAXIA PROGRAMME (Tel: 020 7915 1535) Provides ideas and materials for speech and language therapists to use in their management of children with Articulatory Dyspraxia. Its materials cover most of the oro-motor, sound-producing and sound-sequencing activities which children will need to practice when Dyspraxia is present.

CHILDHOOD SPEECH, LANGUAGE AND LISTENING PROBLEMS
By Patricia McAlleer Hamaguchi (ISBN 0 471 03413 4. Published by John Wiley & Sons, Inc.)
An excellent practical guide for both parents and teachers. After defining each problem it offers some solutions and explains the meanings of the terms used by speech and language therapists. Includes recognition of the difficulties and how they affect the child academically and socially, and tips for helping the child at home.

TOK BACK
(Available from Taskmaster Ltd, Morris Road, Clarendon Park, Leicester LE2 6BR.) Apparatus that hangs over the ears and under the chin. Its use enables students to hear their own speech more clearly.

SPEECH AND LANGUAGE DIFFICULTIES by B. Daines, P.Fleming & C.l Miller (ISBN 0 906730 87 2 Published by NASEN – see Appendix 1 for details.) Provides background information to the problems language-impaired students face in the classroom and useful strategies to help them.

EDITH NORRIE LETTER CASE
Available from Helen Arkell Centre (see Appendix 1) Age suitability: all. Enables the student to gain a better understanding of where each sound is made in the mouth. Its mirror shows the lip movements. Designed by a speech and language therapist, this superb piece of apparatus is a must for those working with students affected by speech difficulties.

DYSLEXIA SPEECH AND LANGUAGE – A Practitioner's Handbook Edited by Margaret Snowling & Joy Stackhouse (ISBN 1 897635 48 6 Whurr Publishers.) Explains the relationship between spoken and written langauge difficulties. Reviews successful methods of teaching reading, spelling & writing.

EARLY COMMUNICATION SKILLS
By Charlottte Lynch & Julia Cooper (ISBN 0 86388 096 7. Published by Winslow Press, Bicester.)
An excellent resource of 100+ communication-based activities for pre-school children for use by teachers and therapists. The copyright-free activity sheets have been designed to be handed to parents for work in the home, & to other key workers to encourage continuity and teamwork. Contents: Pre-verbal skills; Listening – awareness of voice & sound; Vocalisations – Auditory & Speech Discrimination; Auditory/Visual memory – early words.

WORKING WITH CHILDREN'S LANGUAGE
By Jackie Cooke & Diana Williams, edited by Clare Latham (ISBN 0 86388 025 8 Published by Winslow Press, Bicester.)
Contents include theory and activities based on the following: Early language skills, Attention control and listening skills, The role of play, The development of comprehension, The acquisition of expressive language, Perception (including visual, tactile and auditory skills).

COMMUNICATION IN THE CLASSROOM by Lara Schaerf (ISBN 1 873010 87 7 Published by South Kent Community Healthcare NHS Trust.) This handbook for parents, teachers and therapists is very user-friendly and provides plenty of simple ways to encourage communication.

RECEPTIVE LANGUAGE, LISTENING AND COMPREHENSION

LISTENING SKILLS KEYSTAGES 1
ISBN 1 898149 34 8 Age suitability: 5-7 yrs.
LISTENING SKILLS KEYSTAGES 2
ISBN 1 898149 46 1Age suitability: 7-12 yrs.
Written and illustrated by Sandi Rickerby &
Sue Lambert.
(Published by The Questions
Publishing Co. Ltd.) Photocopiable
worksheets of activities which involve
listening & thinking. Repeat each instruction
several times if severe listening difficulties
are present. Omit page 44 as it is too hard for
many students to achieve, especially if
spatial/mathematical difficulties are present.

LISTEN AND DO
(Published by LDA, Duke Street,
Wisbech, Cambs, PE13 2AE Tel: 01945
63441.)
Age range: primary school. Audio tapes and
instruction manual. Provides six 10 minute
lessons that test & expand listening skills,
and which the child can do without adult
supervision. Those with moderate/severe
receptive language difficulties are likely to
need to hear each instruction more than once.

**READING FOR
COMPREHENSION SERIES**
Reading age 7 – 11 yrs
(Published by LDA, Duke Street, Wisbech,
Cambs. PE13 2AE) Boxes of graded cards
which deal with different aspects of
comprehension; e.g. deduction, inference
etc. When Dyslexia is present the student
may have difficulties in using these cards for
they may contain many words that require
higher reading skills. If the student is able to
'build' unknown words then they can be used
as a tool to improve reading comprehension.
The interest level is stated as 8–14 years
though the author has found that the reading
material is not suitable for all students in the
upper part of this age range. The cards can
also be read to the student to improve
auditory skills.

EAROBICS (PC and MAC)
(UK distributor Don Johnston Tel: 01925
241642.) Age suitability: pre-school to adult.

An American auditory training and
phonological awareness computer program.
Various versions suit different ages and
either home or school use.

CENTRAL AUDITORY PROCESSING DISORDER

*This is a very complex condition. One of the
easiest to understand sources of information
is the Internet. To find it, type in the whole
name of the condition or type the letters
CAPD.*

**JOURNAL OF THE AMERICAN
ACADEMY OF AUDIOLOGY:**
Volume 10 Number 6 June 1999 Special
issue: Auditory Processing Disorders in
Children

(ISSN 1050 0545. Published by BC Decker
Inc., 4 Hughson Street South, PO Box 620,
L.C.D.1, Hamilton, Ontario, Canada, L8N
3K7 Tel: 00 1 905 522 7017.)

Contains highly informative articles on
CAPD. A very worthwhile read.

**CHILDHOOD SPEECH, LANGUAGE
AND LISTENING PROBLEMS**
By Patricia McAlleer Hamaguchi
(ISBN 0 471 03413 4. Published by
John Wiley & Sons, Inc.)
This books is written in an easy to
understand way. Contains a section on
Central Auditory Processing Disorder.

**ASSESSMENT AND MANAGEMENT
OF CENTRAL AUDITORY
PROCESSING DISORDERS IN
THE EDUCATIONAL SETTING**
By Teri James Bellis
(ISBN 1 56593 628 0 Singular Publishing
Group, Inc. Available from the UK branch of
this company.)
A very good book on this relatively new
topic to the UK educational scene. It
explains the science of CAPD, its assessment
and management and how to develop a
programme to help those who have this
condition.

DYSPRAXIA

See Appendix 1 for help and support groups for this condition.

DYSCOVER YOURSELF
By Gill Dixon
(Published by the Dyspraxia Foundation, address is in Appendix 1.)
This lovely booklet was designed to be read by children who have Dyspraxia and so give them an understanding of the condition.

PERCEPTUO-MOTOR DIFFICULTIES – Theory and strategies to help children, adolescents and adults
By Dorothy Penso
(ISBN 0 412 39810 9. Published by Stanley Thornes.)
Those affected by perceptuo-motor difficulties are often described as being clumsy. Provides practical information to solve the problems that occur throughout life. Includes information on posture, personal appearance, choosing and sustaining an appropriate career, coping with domestic and child-care activities, leisure pursuits and hobbies.

WATCH ME, I CAN DO IT!
By Neralie Cocks
(ISBN 0 7318 0578 X. Published by Simon & Schuster, Australia but available from UK bookshops.) A very useful book written by an occupational therapist which explains co-ordination difficulties and contains plenty of fun remediation activities that can be done at home or at school.

DEVELOPMENTAL DYSPRAXIA -
Identification & Intervention
A manual for Parents & Professionals
2nd Ed. by Madeleine Portwood
(ISBN 85346 573 9. Published by David Fulton Publishers.)
An excellent book which should be in every school in the country. It provides information on the neurological basis of Dyspraxia, its identification and assessment, effective intervention programmes and much more.

PRAXIS MAKES PERFECT II
Dyspraxia: an essential guide for parents and teachers
Edited by Penny Hunt (ISBN 0 9534344 0 0. Publisher The Dyspraxia Foundation, address is in Appendix 1.)
Recommended Reading for all those interested in Dyspraxia. Includes information on: What is Dyspraxia?, Identification, Assessment and Intervention, Coping with the Behavioural Problems of Children with Developmental Dyspraxia, Low-tech solutions to Classroom Difficulties, Developmental Verbal Dyspraxia, Dealing with Handwriting Problems, Occupational Therapy (the Dyspraxic Child at Secondary School), Physiotherapy and Dyspraxia, Parental Perception of Dyspraxia.

DYSPRAXIA – A GUIDE FOR TEACHERS AND PARENTS
By Kate Ripley, Bob Daines & Jenny Barrett
(ISBN 1 85346 444 9 David Fulton Publishers)
Designed for professionals this book describes the difficulties which face the child who has Dyspraxia and provides strategies for managing the difficulties.

TAKE TIME
by Mary Nash-Wortham & Jean Hunt
(ISBN 1 869981 50 2. Published by The Robinswood Press.)
Designed for teachers. It combines the strategies of movement & language to provide graded development exercises to help language-impaired children who are affected by co-ordination difficulties.

GRADED ACTIVITIES FOR CHILDREN WITH MOTOR DIFFICULTIES
By James R Russell
(ISBN 0 521 33852 2. Published by Cambridge University Press.)
A very useful book for the teacher of primary aged students who have Dyspraxia.

DYSLEXIA AWARENESS
See Appendix 1 for help and support groups for this condition.

SO, YOU THINK YOU'VE GOT PROBLEMS By Rosalind Birket

(ISBN 0 905858 85 9. Published by Egon, Tel: 01462 894498.)
A lovely book designed to be read to the child which explains Dyslexia.

ADULT DYSLEXIA: ASSESSMENT, COUNSELLING & TRAINING
By D McLoughlin, G Fitzgibbon & V Young (ISBN 1 897635 35 4, Whurr Publishers)
Focuses on the difficulties experienced by adults and provides practical advice.

THE GIFT OF DYSLEXIA
By R Davis (0 285 63281 7 Published by Souvenir Press)
Written by a Dyslexic for Dyslexics, this book gives a positive attitude towards Dyslexia. Should be read by all teachers.

DYSLEXIA – PARENTS IN NEED
By Pat Heaton (ISBN 1897635 73 7, Whurr Publishers.) Includes information on the signs of Dyslexia and how families react to the diagnosis and cope with the difficulties it presents.

DYSLEXIA – A PARENT'S SURVIVAL GUIDE by Christine Ostler
(ISBN 1 869866 06 1. Published by Ammonite Books.)
This easy-to-read practical guide offers advice for parents.

BRITISH DYSLEXIA ASSOCIATION PUBLICATIONS
The Dyslexia Handbook (published yearly) provides up-to-date information on Dyslexia. 'Dyslexia – Early Help, Better Future' is a very simple to follow short video. 'Dyslexia in the Primary Classroom' is a video and manual aimed at staff development for teachers which highlights the problems and suggest appropriate teaching strategies. 'Dyslexia: Signposts to Success' is a guide for adults who have Dyslexia.

OVERCOMING DYSLEXIA
By Beve Hornsby (ISBN 0 09 181320. Published by Vermilion.) An easy-to-read guide for families and teachers which is full of practical advice.

A TASTE OF DYSLEXIA
Presented by Dr Ginny Stacey (Available from: Oxfordshire Dyslexia Association, 41 Golders Close, Ickford, Bucks, HP18 9JA)

This video contains a series of activities that have been devised to generate, temporarily, Dyslexia effects in the minds of non-Dyslexic people.

LEARNING AND LEARNING STYLES

PEOPLE TYPES AND TIGER STRIPES
by Gordon Lawrence (ISBN 0 935652 16 7.)
This fascinating book explains people's behaviour into sixteen types and gives practical advice on how to adapt your teaching style and environment to fit your student's needs.

TEACHING FOR THE TWO-SIDED MIND by Linda Verlee Williams
(ISBN 0 671 62239 0.)
Teachers, parents, undergraduates and all those interested in education will find this a fascinating book to read and for many it will open up an entirely new way of thinking, teaching and learning. It contains a wealth of practical information.

THE LEARNING REVOLUTION
by Gordon Dryden & Dr Jeannette Vos (ISBN 0 905553 43 8.
An excellent and fascinating book to read which contains lots of practical advice on more effective learning strategies which range from playing music in the background whilst studying to tape-assisted reading techniques.

USEFUL COMPUTER PROGRAMS

All are suitable for home and school use for with children. Those also suitable for use with teenagers and adults are marked with an *.

BECTA provide free up-to-date information on computer soft/hardware, Website www.becta.org.uk or Tel: 01203 416994. **Teem**: www.teem.org.uk provide teachers' reviews of software. **Semerc**: www.semerc.co.uk Their catalogue includes a large range of software suitable for special needs students.

CREATIVE WRITING PROGRAMS
STORYMAKER (PC)
(Published by SPA, PO Box 59, Tewkesbury, England, GL20 6AB Tel: 01684 833 700 Fax: 01584 833 718.) Age suitability: primary + lower secondary. Students can add objects to a very colourful cartoon-style main picture based on a variety of themes; e.g. pirates, and then add captions to parts of the picture.

CLICKER (PC & Archimedes)
(Published by: Crick computing, 1 The Avenue, Spinney Hill, Northampton, NN3 6BA Tel: 01604 671 691.) Various versions, each provides grids on screen which display words/phrases/pictures. Can use the mouse to click on the box of their choice and the words etc. appear on the screen. Its very easy to make your own grids. Free Clicker grids at website www.cricksoft.com/cgfl

STORYBOOK WEAVER (PC)
(Available from Rickett Educational Media, Great Western House, Langport, Somerset, TA10 9YU Tel: 01458 256 636 Fax: 01458 253 646.) A very inexpensive and colourful program. The 'Classic' version allows the student to click on a picture of the word and see it appear as text.

MICROSOFT PUBLISHER (PC) *
A relatively easy-to-use desktop publishing program. Can be bought via computer magazines and some High Street shops.
The following are talking word processors:
TALKING PENDOWN (PC/Acorn)
(Published by Longman Logotron, 124 Cambridge Science Park, Milton Road, Cambridge, CB4 4ZS.)
WRITE OUTLOUD (PC)
(Published by Don Johnston, see page 11.)

SPELLINGS/PHONICS
XAVIER EDUCATIONAL SOFTWARE
(Dept. of Psychology, University College North Wales, Bangor, Gwynedd, LL57 2DG.) Produce a range of good software for BBC, Archimedes and PC. The author particularly likes their Magic E program.
WORDSHARK 2L *
PC & Nimbus (White Space Ltd., 41 Mall Road, London, W6 9DG Tel/Fax: 0181 748 5927.) A brilliant program that has 23 games that teach various phonic blends and skills. Needs a soundcard.

READING
SHERSTON SOFTWARE LTD.
(Angel House, Sherston, Malmesbury, Wiltshire SN16 0LH.) Produce some very colourful & fun programs which talk; e.g. Ridiculous Rhymes (7+ yrs) the one about Brussels Sprouts is my favourite, Rosie & Jim Talking Activities (3-6 years), Talking Nursery Rhymes (4-6 yrs), Sherston Naughty Stories (5-7yrs), Rusty Dreamer (8-14yrs) reading combined with solving a mystery, Oxford Reading Tree Talking Software (5-7 yrs) cover many of the books in the reading scheme + a clipart program and activity software that reinforces phonics. Non-fiction available too; e.g. 'Look! Hear! Talking Topics' (5-7yrs). Also available are a lovely Clip Art Collection series of disks on a variety of topics.

TALKING RHYMES
(Topologika Software Tel: 01326 377771.) The student has to build a jigsaw of a nursery rhyme. Words are sung/spoken by the computer.

ENGLISH LANGUAGE WORK
Matti Mole's Summer Holiday (software) (Published by Sherston – see above) Covers punctuation, plurals, verbs etc.
Spelling & Grammar (book) (Published by Ladybird ISBN 0 7214 1854 6) Available from High Street shops.) Covers verbs, nouns, adjectives, building sentences, punctuation, spelling & grammar rules. A very easy-to-use & colourful reference book.

PREDICTIVE LEXICONS

These computer programs work with most word processors and guess what the student wants to write, the student then presses a single key and the computer types in the text. Prophet (PC Windows 3.1, 95 only, from Ace Centre Tel: 01865 63508); Co-writer (PC, talks, puts text into a window first – this can be irritating for the brighter student: from Don Johnston, Tel: 01925 241642); Penfriend (PC/Acorn, talks, can be used with Clicker 3: from Design Concept Tel 0131 668 2000); Texthelp! (talks, from: TextHELP! Systems Ltd, Antrim, Northern Ireland Tel: 01849 428105).

TEACHING SCHEMES

DYSLEXIA STILE Age suitability: 9+ (All Stile materials are available from: LDA, Duke St., Wisbech, Cambs, PE13 2AE.) Structured programme which uses the Stile apparatus which has to purchased separately. Developed in consultation with the Dyslexia Institute it provides a fun way to reinforce spelling and grammar rules.
TOE BY TOE (ages 7+) by Cowling & Cowling (ISBN 0 9522564 0 1 from: 'Toe by Toe', 8 Green Road, Baildon, W Yorks, BD17 5HL Tel:01274 598807.) Very effective workbook that improves reading and spelling using phonic based methods. Can be used part at home and part at school. May not suit students who dislike repetitive lesson format.
RIME TIME by H. Bellamy & S. Dart (Published by Crossbow, 41 Sawpit Lane, Brocton, Staffs, ST17 0TE Tel: 01785 660902.) Age: upper primary + secondary . A comprehensive photocopiable resource for rescuing literacy skills, based on research by Goswami & others. A proven success in the classroom. Contains illustrated worksheets, spelling lists, dictations and diagnostic test.
BEAT DYSLEXIA ACTIVITY PACKS By Celia Stone, Elizabeth Franks & Myra Nicholson (LDA, Duke St., Wisbech, Cambs PE13 2AE.) Suitable age: 5+. Each pack concentrates on different sound patterns and contains 50+ photocopiable worksheets plus a cassette tape and press-out letters which provide a simplified way for students to learn phonics, spelling, reading and writing.

HANDWRITING

ERGONOMIC DESKS & CHAIRS (Supplier: Sebel Design, C2 The Courtyard, Alban Park, St Albans, Herts, AL4 0LA.) Extremely comfortable. Desks do not have a smooth surface. They are adjustable so that they can be at an angle or flat. Note: desktop has a rough surface.
ROSEMARY SASSOON BOOKS She has written a variety of books. Leopard Learning (Tel: 01452 812271) publish **'Practical guide to children's handwriting'** A useful book for parents and teachers of early years children. **'Handwriting – the way to teach it'** Covers all aspects of primary school teaching. Its companion **'Handwriting – a new perspective'** is most useful for special needs teachers. **'Helping with Handwriting'** (ISBN 07195 71359) published by John Murray is aimed at secondary school students
HANDWRITING HELPLINE by J Alston & J Taylor (ISBN 1 872177 09 3. Published by Dextral Books.) This book is useful if the handwriting difficulty is not severe.
Philip & Tacey, North Way, Andover, Hants, SP10 5BA supply sloping desks (that sit on a table) and exercise books.

PLANNING & ORGANISATION

PLANNING & ORGANISATION SOLUTIONS by Jan Poustie (ISBN 1 901544 81 8. Published by Next Generation; see page A24 for address.) Age suitability: 7+ yrs. Suitable for use by parents/professionals/other adults. Provides simple, effective strategies for planning many areas of life and the curriculum; e.g. language, writing, revision, decision-making, resources/strategies that help in the workplace/home etc. Includes a host of photocopiable sheets.
GET AHEAD by Vanda North & Tony Buzan (ISBN 1 874374 00 7 Buzan Centres, 54 Parkstone Road, Poole, Dorset, BH15 2PX. Tel: 01202 674 676.) A very easy introduction to Mind Mapping. It and other materials on Mind Mapping; e.g. audio/video tapes, and more complex books are also available from the same publisher.

TEACHING SCHEMES

SPELLING MADE EASY
by Violet Brand (Egon Publishers Ltd., Royston Road, Herts, SG7 6NW.) A set of good, easy-to-use, phonic based materials.

THE HICKEY MULTISENSORY LANGUAGE COURSE
edited by Augur & Briggs, revised and updated 2nd Ed.
Age suitability: all. (ISBN 1 870332 52 0 Published by Whurr.) An invaluable very carefully structured multisensory teaching programme. Is for specialist teacher use only.

ALPHA TO OMEGA
by Dr Bevé Hornsby and others (Heinemann Educational, Halley Court, Jordan Hill, Oxford, OX2 8EJ.) A very highly-regarded phonics-based programme. (Main book, work-sheets, flash-cards). Suitable for: teachers/informed parents.

MULTI-SENSORY LEARNING
(Earlstrees Court, Earlstrees Road, Corby, Northants, NN17 4HH.) Produce the Multi-Sensory Learning Structured Literacy Course – (very wide ranging photocopiable worksheets + equipment) which can be used by both professionals & parents.

TEACHING STRATEGIES
These are good starting points for teachers intending to specialise in SpLD.

HOW TO DETECT AND MANAGE DYSLEXIA by Philomena Ott (Published by Heinemann ISBN 0 435 10419 5.)
Provides comprehensive information on Dyslexia, its current management & resource stockists and history of Dyslexia. Motor functioning recommendations are sometimes not comprehensive/flexible enough.

DAY-TO-DAY DYSLEXIA IN THE CLASSROOM by Joy Pollock & Elisabeth Waller (ISBN 0 415 11132 3. Published by Routledge.)

SPECIFIC LEARNING DIFFICULTIES (DYSLEXIA) - A Teachers Guide 2nd Ed.
by Margaret Crombie (ISBN 1 900506 02 5 Ann Arbor Publishers.)

SPELLING & READING

PHONIC RHYME TIME
by Mary Nash-Wortham, Age suitability: 7+ (ISBN 1 869981 47 2. Published by The Robinswood Press.) Resource book for teachers/speech therapists. 200+ fun, attractively presented rhymes cover all phonic positions.

WORDGAMES FOR WINDOWS
(Published by SPA, PO Box 59, Tewkesbury, England, GL20 6AB.) A lovely, very easy-to-use computer program (for PC). Produces wordsearches and crosswords. You type in the clues and the answers; and the computer prints it out. Can be a great incentive to practise spellings, sentence construction etc.

SOUND LINKAGE: AN INTEGRATED PROGRAMME FOR OVERCOMING READING DIFFICULTIES
By Peter Hatcher (ISBN 1 897635 31 1, Published by Whurr.) A structured easy-to-use system which teaches a variety of phonological skills. Has a test of phonological awareness.

The following are available from LDA, Duke St., Wisbech, Cambs, PE13 2AE.

THE PHONIC REFERENCE FILE
by Gill Cotterell. Checklist of basic sounds, phonic word lists for teaching specific rules, sounds and diagnostic spelling test.

THE LDA WORDBUILDING BOX
A boxed set of wooden lower-case letters approx. 2 cms high (vowels red, consonants blue) and grids to put them on.

EARLY YEARS SPELLING & READING

BEFORE ALPHA by Bevé Hornsby
(Published by Souvenir Press ISBN 0 285 63327 9.) A structured programme of games, activities, songs & stories which helps develop language skills for the under-fives.

LETTERLAND (from W. H. Smith)
For pre-school and early primary children. Via books, workbooks, videos etc. it teaches the sounds the letters make in a fun way. *Also see Useful Computer Programs Section, page A32 of this appendix.*

Index

(This index covers Chapters 1–10 and the Appendices. The letter *A* followed by
an italicised number, refers to an entry in one of the Appendices)